W9-DHN-042

Y͏ ͏ ͏es

Your Money Milestones

A Guide to Making the 9 Most Important
Financial Decisions of Your Life

Moshe A. Milevsky, Ph.D.

Vice President, Publisher: Tim Moore
Associate Publisher and Director of Marketing: Amy Neidlinger
Executive Editor: Jim Boyd
Editorial Assistant: Pamela Boland
Development Editor: Russ Hall
Operations Manager: Gina Kanouse
Senior Marketing Manager: Julie Phifer
Publicity Manager: Laura Czaja
Assistant Marketing Manager: Megan Colvin
Cover Designer: Alan Clements
Managing Editor: Kristy Hart
Project Editor: Julie Anderson
Copy Editor: Apostrophe Editing Services
Proofreader: Leslie Joseph
Indexer: WordWise Publishing Services LLC
Compositor: Jake McFarland
Manufacturing Buyer: Dan Uhrig

Publishing as FT Press

Upper Saddle River, New Jersey 07458

This book is sold with the understanding that neither the author nor the publisher is engaged in rendering legal, accounting, or other professional services or advice by publishing this book. Each individual situation is unique. Thus, if legal or financial advice or other expert assistance is required in a specific situation, the services of a competent professional should be sought to ensure that the situation has been evaluated carefully and appropriately. The author and the publisher disclaim any liability, loss, or risk resulting directly or indirectly, from the use or application of any of the contents of this book.

FT Press offers excellent discounts on this book when ordered in quantity for bulk purchases or special sales. For more information, please contact U.S. Corporate and Government Sales, 1-800-382-3419, corpsales@pearsontechgroup.com. For sales outside the U.S., please contact International Sales at international@pearson.com.

Company and product names mentioned herein are the trademarks or registered trademarks of their respective owners.

First Printing January 2010

ISBN-10: 0-13-702910-1
ISBN-13: 978-0-13-702910-5

Pearson Education LTD.
Pearson Education Australia PTY, Limited.
Pearson Education Singapore, Pte. Ltd.
Pearson Education North Asia, Ltd.
Pearson Education Canada, Ltd.
Pearson Educatión de Mexico, S.A. de C.V.
Pearson Education—Japan
Pearson Education Malaysia, Pte. Ltd.

Library of Congress Cataloging-in-Publication Data

Milevsky, Moshe Arye, 1967-
  Your money milestones : a guide to making the 9 most important financial decisions in your life / Moshe A. Milevsky.
      p. cm.
  ISBN-13: 978-0-13-702910-5 (hardback : alk. paper)
  ISBN-10: 0-13-702910-1
  1. Finance, Personal. 2. Finance, Personal—Decision making. 3. Investments. I. Title.
  HG179.M4592 2010
  332.024—dc22
                          2009034907

"...A broader view of wealth may indeed be taken for some purposes... and perhaps it may be convenient to have a term which will include it as part of personal wealth in a broader use. Pursuing the lines indicated by Adam Smith (1784) in *The Wealth of Nations*, we may define personal wealth so as to include all those energies, faculties, and habits which directly contribute to making people industrially efficient...."

—Alfred Marshall (1890) *Principles of Economics*, Chapter II.

Dedicated to my genuine pensions,
Dahlia, Natalie, Maya, and Zoe.

Contents

Acknowledgments

I would like to start by thanking the various people who claim to have read my previous book: *Are You a Stock or a Bond? Create Your Own Pension Plan for a Secure Financial Future* (FT Press 2008) and then proceeded to complain that although they liked the general idea, I *should have* used the opportunity to discuss the many other financial issues people face over their life cycle, not just pensions and retirement income planning.

I directly blame them for having to break my promise to my family—sworn during the frigid Canadian winter of 2008—that I would hold off writing yet another book for at least a few years.

This book was researched and written during the 2008/2009 academic year, while I was on sabbatical from York University (in Toronto) and spent time as a Visiting Fellow at the University of Technology, Sydney, Australia, and a Visiting Scholar at the Insurance and Risk Management Department at the Wharton School, University of Pennsylvania, Philadelphia. I am grateful to both of these institutions for their hospitality and the faculty for insights and fruitful conversations.

Likewise, I would like to thank Jim Boyd, Julie Anderson, and everyone at FT Press who helped convert a rough manuscript into a finished book. I would also like to express my gratitude to Anna Abaimova, Faisal Habib, Huaxiong Huang, Kevin Lin, Alexandra Macqueen, and Tom Salisbury, all affiliated with The QWeMA Group in Toronto for taking time from their regular obligations to help answer questions, collect information, and design calculators for our Dynamic Life Cycle project. In particular I would like to recognize Alexandra Macqueen who helped with actual research and editing of this manuscript. Along the same lines, I am indebted to my life partner and wife Edna, who offered critical comments on every aspect of the manuscript (and almost everything else I do).

Finally, I would like to take this opportunity to apologize to my four daughters who continue to put up with a father who is obviously not quite normally distributed. I promise this book is it for a while....

About the Author

Moshe A. Milevsky, Ph.D. is a tenured finance professor at the Schulich School of Business at York University (www.yorku.ca) in Toronto, Canada, and the executive director of the nonprofit IFID Centre (www.ifid.ca). He is also the president and CEO of The QWeMA Group (www.qwema.ca), a software company that develops intellectual property and numerical algorithms for the financial services industry. He also writes a monthly column for *Research Magazine* that is read by financial advisors and planners in North America.

Moshe is a well-known public speaker and has delivered keynote lectures and seminars in Europe, South America, the Far East, and the UK. In June 2009, he was a main platform speaker for MDRT's annual meeting. He has consulted for global insurance companies and pension funds including the Florida State Board of Administration's (FSBA) retirement plan. He is currently a member of a variety of corporate advisory councils. To date he has published seven books, more than 50 peer-reviewed research papers, and more than 100 personal finance articles on the topic of insurance, investments, pensions, retirement, and annuities.

Moshe received two National Magazine (Canada) awards in 2003 for his popular-press writing and received a Graham and Dodd scroll award from the CFA Institute for a 2006 research article in the *Financial Analysts Journal*. In the summer of 2002, he was elected a Fellow of the Fields Institute for Research in Mathematical Sciences, and in September 2008, he was given a lifetime achievement award from the Retirement Income Industry Association (RIIA). In May 2009, he was named to *Investment Advisor* magazine's IA25 list of most influential people in the financial advisory business.

Moshe's previous book *Are You a Stock or a Bond? Create Your Own Pension Plan for a Secure Financial Future* was published by FT Press in September 2008 and is available in fine bookstores everywhere.

Prologue: Financial Deicide

From early November 2007 to mid-March 2009, I watched in horror as about half of my family's financial net worth, made up mostly of common stocks and mutual funds in our retirement investment accounts, disappeared into thin air. This wasn't a trivial sum of money: It was in the high six digits. It is far more than my wife or I can possibly earn in any given year. Like many other investors around the world who experienced similar losses, I managed to achieve this stunning feat by complying with every known morsel of established financial planning wisdom. *I lost hundreds of thousands of dollars by doing everything exactly right.*

I didn't own much in the way of speculative penny stocks, nor did I take a flyer on some exotic junk bond funds, commodity derivatives, or collateralized debt obligations. Instead, I built an ultra-low-cost, globally-diversified portfolio that included what were (at the time) some of the most solid, well-respected, and best-known companies—like American International Group (aka AIG), Lehman Brothers, General Motors, Nortel, and so on. I bought and I held.

This, of course, is exactly what the mainstream financial planning and investment industry had been preaching for years. I know this because I have taught it to my undergraduate business students for almost 20 years.

The spectacular destruction of value that I and many others experienced has caused many investors to question the underlying premises of almost everything they've been taught about investment risk, asset allocation, wealth management, and financial planning. And, although markets have recovered since the March 2009 lows, the financial situation is still precarious. Indeed, the mainstream financial news media—including the venerable *The Wall Street Journal* and the *Economist* magazine—have joined the backlash against modern portfolio theory and the perceived wisdom of decades. Numerous financial commentators are questioning the views that financial markets are efficient, or that stocks outperform bonds in the long run, or that asset allocation and portfolio diversification are appropriate strategies for individual investors. Indeed, entire books have recently been published with the sole purpose of arguing that we've all been wrong for the last quarter century. Financial heroes and their money gurus are being slaughtered.

Spectators to this "financial deicide" are thus left to wonder: "Okay. So, what am I supposed to do with my money? If all the received wisdom is out the window then how do I make financial decisions?"

Two Opposing Views of the Future

Let's step back for a minute to get a wider view. Today, there are two prevailing and very opposing philosophies for thinking about how to navigate the world of stock prices and interest rates. You can think of them as the *roulette* approach on one side, versus the *nuclear* approach on the other.

According to the *roulette* view, estimating your portfolio's and investment's future value is akin to predicting the odds of getting red versus black, or odd versus even, on the roulette wheel at the casino. That is, given sufficient data about the previous behavior and possible outcomes of the market (or the wheel), you can predict the odds of success or failure—and make money—with reasonable confidence. In fact, casino managers at Las Vegas and Atlantic City have a long list of mathematicians and statisticians who are supposed to be bounced from the tables, on sight. Apparently they are just too good to be allowed to play.

In contrast, the *nuclear* approach asks us to consider the odds of a nuclear accident—similar to Three Mile Island or Chernobyl—occurring in a given time period. But this problem is quite different from calculating the odds of red versus black. You could claim that over the 60 years since the advent of nuclear energy—which is 21,900 days—we've had accidents on two of those days; ergo, the odds of disaster must be 2 in 21,900. However, this argument is ridiculous. It is impossible to predict a nuclear accident using any statistical or historical model, and no one seriously tries. Instead, unpredictability is a given in the nuclear environment, and risk is managed in various ways.

Now, back to stock markets: For many years, financial researchers—myself included—firmly believed that markets were like roulette wheels (if you'll forgive the analogy), in which future odds and probabilities can be derived and stated with confidence.

Now, though, many are starting to wonder if stock markets are better described like nuclear events (if you'll forgive *that* analogy). Accidents and meltdowns can occur at any time and without much warning. But if markets are more like nuclear events than roulette wheels, then historical relationships might not be very relevant for interpreting and predicting the future at all, and finding a way to navigate this reframed future requires new approaches.

In light of this dilemma, this book is an attempt to go back to arithmetic basics to provide some guidance on how to make financial decisions. Moreover, this advice doesn't require you to assume very much statistically about the world around us, *other than that the future is unpredictable.* Working from the nuclear metaphor of uncertainty (versus risk), this book offers a guide—based on arithmetic operations that are no more complicated than addition, subtraction, multiplication, and (most important) division—to help you properly and confidently manage the nine most important financial decisions you will make in life.

Aiming for the Best Outcome

The tools I give you for making financial decisions are, as I've said, extremely basic. But the approach I suggest is not simply "use arithmetic to solve personal financial problems." Instead, in thinking about ways to move forward, I was inspired by another group of scientists working—and succeeding—in an environment of uncertainty. And so, there's one more idea I want to introduce now, as it will shape discussions in the rest of the book.

As I complete this manuscript in July 2009, we are closing in on the 40th anniversary of the U.S. astronauts' first walk on the moon. In the late 1950s, when the U.S. space industry was racing the Soviets to dominate the "final frontier," a group of research engineers developed and ultimately refined a new branch of science now known as Dynamic Control Theory (DCT). This theory was created in response to the formidable challenge facing the engineers, who had to launch a rocket far into space without managing or even knowing many of the conditions in the atmosphere and beyond. Boiled down to its intuitive essence, DCT—which is now taught in engineering and mathematics departments all over the world—is a framework that helps decision makers carefully utilize the levers and knobs that are available for adjustment, while openly recognizing the multiple variables over which they have no influence (and hence for which no levers or knobs are available).

In applying DCT, one of the key steps is scoping out all the factors that can be quantified for a given decision, and then selecting an objective function that weighs the relative importance of each, to evaluate how good a proposed solution is. When this broad framework has been established, the engineering team can work from controllable variables and quantified factors to make the best possible decisions in the face of unknown factors and uncontrollable variables. DCT is both powerful and useful because it acknowledges the substantial randomness that you face over long periods of time and provides a decision-making mechanism that ultimately tries to maximize the odds of a regretless outcome.

I think the DCT metaphor is apt for personal finance because one of my core beliefs is that a large part of our financial future is uncontrollable. Great wealth, good fortune, and economic success can be influenced by random luck, uncanny timing, and other factors outside our immediate authority. In fact, you can argue that even for the brightest and hardest working among us, the bulk of our financial successes and economic failures is unpredictable. If this is true, when making financial decisions, all there is to do is aim for the best outcome across the remaining minority of possible scenarios you can foresee and control.

Accordingly, the mission of this book (so to speak) is to provide you with a useful guide to making milestone financial decisions through your entire life cycle. Where applicable, I include links to online calculators so that you can work through and quantify issues for your own life. (All the calculators can be found at www.quema.ca.) Each chapter in this book builds toward a comprehensive foundation. Nevertheless, each chapter, which explores a different financial milestone, can be read and understood independently. Taken as a whole, this book is designed to explain how to take the lessons of DCT and insights from human capital thinking and apply them to the most important financial milestones in our lives—leaving you with fresh context for understanding and successfully navigating your own personal financial journey.

Introduction:
Human Capital: Your Greatest Asset

Before you go any farther, I'd like to challenge you to complete a simple exercise. Ready?

Take out a blank sheet of paper, and draw a straight line right down the center, splitting the sheet into two equal parts. Now write "My Assets" on the top-left side of the paper and at the top right, "My Liabilities." In the language of financial accounting, I am asking you to create a *personal balance sheet* that lists the value of everything you own and everything you owe.

On the right side of your personal balance sheet—which lists all your debts and liabilities—you should include the amount you owe on credit cards, consumer loans, mortgages, and anything else you relate to as a financial obligation. On the left side you should list the value of all your assets, including money in bank accounts, traded stocks, savings bonds, pension accounts, equity in a small business, the value of a car, and any other items of value you own.

Now, after you list all your assets and liabilities, add them up to get summary numbers. What is the value of everything you own, and what is the total value of what you owe?

Finally, subtract what you *owe* from what you *own*. The resulting number—whether positive or negative—is your *net worth*. Getting you to think about and then calculate this important number is the starting point for everything that follows in this book. Through this exercise, I want you to consider what you are truly worth in stark economic terms.

Now, you may have already done an exercise like this in the past. Perhaps you've created a personal or household net worth statement, and at this point, you're thinking that you aren't going to learn anything from this chapter (and maybe even the entire book) that you don't already know. Except hang on, because I'm about to tell you that *you probably did the exercise incorrectly and omitted the most important item and the most valuable asset you own.*

How so? Well, let's take a look at what happens when I ask my undergraduate business students to undertake exactly the same exercise.

As you've probably figured out by now, my day job involves teaching undergraduate and graduate business courses at York University in Toronto. My favorite subject to teach is a 12-week undergraduate course on the topic of wealth management. When I start this course anew each semester, on the first day of class, before I discuss the syllabus, the course textbook, or the final exam schedule, I ask each student to prepare their own personal balance sheet.

Now, their situations are probably different from yours. To start, they're typically only about 20 years old. But already, a large portion of them have substantial debt obligations: Many of them have taken out student loans in the range of $10,000 to $40,000. In this way, my students are like college grads in the United States, in which the average student loan balance was $20,100 in 2007.[1] To be sure, these students might not need to pay back their loans for many years, and the loans might not be accruing any interest while they are in school, but all of them recognize their loans as liabilities with a current value.[2] My students also report having a substantial amount of credit card debt. On average, they report slightly more than $3,100 as a revolving balance on their personal balance sheet. These numbers are broadly reflective of credit card indebtedness for that age category, according to Sallie Mae, a U.S. student loan company.[3] However, unlike their student loans, on these liabilities the interest clock is ticking daily—and rates can approach 20 percent, and even 30 percent, for some bank and department store cards.

My students also often include consumer loans on their balance sheets because many of them owe money on cars they have financed or funds borrowed from roommates, parents, cousins, and the occasional loan shark. In sum: Most of them have plenty of debts and liabilities.

---

1. Reed, *Student Debt and the Class of 2007.*
2. In Canada, average student loan debt for a graduate with a bachelor's degree is $22,800 (2007 Canadian dollars). Bayard and Greenlee, "Graduating in Canada."
3. From *How undergraduate students use credit cards: Sallie Mae's national study of usage rates and trends 2009.*

When they get to the left side of their personal balance sheets, they often admit to having difficulties finding any values to include. As you might suspect, at the age of 20 many of them don't have much in the way of traditional financial assets. They don't own houses. They don't have any stocks or bonds. They don't own any mutual funds, Treasury bills, or savings bonds, and they certainly don't have any pension accounts. Remember, some of these kids aren't yet of legal drinking age!

Some of my students include the little bit of money they have in a savings account at the local bank or perhaps the value of the bicycle they use to ride to class. In fact, sometimes a hand will go up, and a student will ask me if he should include the newly-increased credit limit on his MasterCard or Visa on the left side as a financial asset. (Note: The answer is no.)

Now, you can view this exercise—either the one I posed to you at the start of this chapter, or the one I give my new students each semester— as a rather private, possibly intrusive, and perhaps even depressing assignment. But as I am working through the creation of their personal balance sheets with my students, I make it clear that I do *not* want them to hand their sheets in to me at the end of class. I don't want to make them uncomfortable. I'm not trying to pry into their personal financial affairs. My goal, as I've said, is just to get them to compute what they think their net worth is by subtracting the value of the financial assets they have identified from the value of their financial liabilities—but they get to keep the resulting number to themselves, just like you do.

Is That Glass Half-Empty or Half-Full? Valuing Human Capital

When my students are done creating their initial balance sheet, I ask them two additional questions. You can think about the answers to these questions, too. The first is: *Do you think your personal balance sheet will look better ten years from now?* When I ask this question in class, virtually every hand goes up in response. My students are optimistic about their career prospects and hence their future personal balance sheet. I then ask, *How many of you got a zero or negative number for your net worth on the balance sheet today?* Be *honest now.* Reluctantly, and slowly, the vast majority of the juniors and seniors raise their hands.

At this point, if they were a publicly traded company, with this admission of a zero or negative net worth number, they would immediately be deemed insolvent or even bankrupt. In fact, the smattering of students—from a group of 60—who do not raise their hands are usually exchange students (who perhaps didn't understand the exercise) or are the children of wealthy parents (maybe in Dubai?) who don't have any liabilities.

Now here's the twist: I then announce to my students that based on their responses it seems to me they did the exercise all wrong, and they probably answered both questions incorrectly. I tell them that I know they are relying on their previous studies of business accounting, using bookkeeping techniques or Financial Accounting Standards Board guidelines, to create their personal balance sheets. Much to their surprise, I suggest they are undoubtedly missing the most important item and most valuable asset class they own, and they are forgetting the reason they enrolled in school and have incurred all their student loan debt.

And now back to you—what my students have undoubtedly left off their list of assets is the same thing that's probably missing from yours—the value of what economists call *human capital.*

But what is human capital? At the young age of 20, as I've said, my students generally have little in the way of traditional financial capital. But they do have 40 to 50 years of salary, bonus, and wage income ahead of them. One powerful way to consider this future income is to view it as an asset like a gold mine or oil well with 50 more years of reserves.

Think of it this way: If you own a well or mine, you probably cannot extract more than a small fraction of the reserves in any given year. (And it might be very costly to do so.) However, *this asset has substantial value today*. I'll say this again to make sure it's clear: *The most valuable asset class for most people during most of their working years is their human capital*. Not just college kids in their early 20s or graduate students in their late 20s—this applies to you in your 30s, 40s, and even 50s and 60s.

Human capital should be viewed in exactly the same way as a gold mine or oil well: It has a tangible present value—right now—even if it takes many more years before you see six-figure cash flows from it. Accordingly, they should include the estimated current value of human capital to create what I call a *holistic personal balance sheet*. And I'm giving the same instruction to you. Although you might be slightly older than 20, your human capital is likely the largest asset on your personal balance sheet throughout most of your life.

Table I.1 shows how a holistic personal balance sheet might look.

TABLE I.1 Holistic Personal Balance Sheet and Net Worth Calculation

My Assets	**My Liabilities**
Explicit Financial Capital	- Visible Debt and Liabilities
+ Implicit Financial Capital[4]	- Estimated Hidden Liabilities
+ Estimated Human Capital	
= Total Capital	= Holistic Net Worth

But how do you come up with an estimate of the value of your human capital?

To help my students arrive at a reasonable number, I give them a follow-up assignment to visit our campus alumni office or career center to collect data on how much people earn after they graduate from school. This information is also widely available online (on websites such as collegegrad.com), broken down by college major, geographical region, and sometimes even by school grades. As their second assignment, I ask my students to calculate the present value (that is, the value today) of the next 50 years of their total after-tax compensation, including wages, salary, and bonus.

Presto! My students come back to their next class a week later and joyfully declare that their human capital is currently worth millions of dollars. Indeed, even using conservative assumptions for

---

4. I define *Implicit Financial Capital* as the present value of all defined benefit pensions, Social Security (or Canada Pension Plan) benefits, and other illiquid entitlements to future cash flows that you can't sell or trade in the secondary market but that you have earned by virtue of your past labor market participation and are guaranteed to receive after retirement for your lifetime. My students, generally speaking, do not have any implicit financial capital—yet.

salary growth rates and discount rates, coming from one of the better undergraduate business schools in the country, their human capital values are well into the seven digits.

I've included a human capital calculator at www.qwema.ca, so you can try this exercise, too. What is your human capital worth? After you estimate and include your human capital, what does your holistic personal balance sheet look like?

Mark Yourself to Market

At this point, my students and you have learned lesson number one from this book, which I call *mark yourself to market*. If you worked through the calculations to estimate the value of your human capital, you have also learned to properly identify and sum the current value of all your future cash flows, and not just the financial assets you have today. In so doing, you have created a holistic personal balance sheet that takes into account both your explicit financial capital (the traditional financial assets you own today) and your human capital.

Let's take a closer look at valuing human capital. Using data provided by the Current Population Survey from the U.S. Census, I estimate that at the age of 25—with the potential of 40 to 50 more years of labor income ahead—the human capital of a college graduate (not necessarily a business student) can range anywhere between $540,000 and $1,700,000 on an after-tax basis.[5] (These numbers are rough estimates based on a number of embedded assumptions,[6] but they're in the right ballpark.) Ten years later, at the age of 35, that same college graduate has an implied human capital value between $560,000 and $1,600,000. At the age of 45 the range is $500,000 to

---

5. In Canada, the median value of human capital at the age of 25 after completing an undergraduate degree is roughly $1.3 million, assuming a discount rate of 3.5 percent. Data source: payscale.com; QWeMA Group calculations.

6. In generating these estimates, I included only income from earnings; I adjusted for tax using average 2008 effective tax rates; and I assumed income from employment to age 75. Lower estimates are based on 40th percentile income (only 40 percent of people have incomes lower than this) and a discount rate of 6 percent; upper estimates are based on 90th percentile income (90 percent of people have incomes lower than this) and a discount rate of 3.5 percent.

$1,400,000, and—perhaps surprisingly—at 65 the remaining value of human capital is between $160,000 and $480,000.[7] I want to underscore that these derived values are not formal measures of net worth and do not, as I've said, take into account any traditional financial capital, such as the value of pensions or Social Security entitlements. My human capital estimates simply represent the present (that is, discounted) value of the wages and income you can expect to receive during your remaining working years.

Using this methodology and data from the Bureau of Labor Statistics, I can provide estimates of human capital based on specific professions and for individuals who have more than a college degree. For example, at the age of 25, an average physician's human capital is worth approximately $2.7 million, an average lawyer's human capital is worth approximately $2.1 million, and an average civil engineer's human capital is worth approximately $1.4 million. An average plumber's human capital is worth $960,000, and an average baker's human capital (yes, the Bureau of Labor Statistics has a category for bakers!) is worth $520,000. (You will have the opportunity to delve into these differences by occupation further in Chapter 1 ("Is the Long-Term Value of an Education Worth the Short-Term Cost?"), that looks at the true value of an education.)

Is This a Cynic's Value or True Worth?

Now, you might think it rather cynical to evaluate training, education, and lifelong learning in purely financial terms. In contrast, I believe the notion of human capital is ultimately a deeply encouraging one. For example, many of my undergraduate and graduate students find comfort in the notion that their holistic net worth contains this substantial hidden asset. I am also not the first or the only university professor to emphasize the importance and value of human capital. The most celebrated economist in the study of human capital is Nobel laureate Dr. Gary Becker, from the University of Chicago. He

---

7. See footnote #5 for the Canadian values.

popularized thinking about the value of education as an investment in human capital in his classic *Human Capital: A Theoretical and Empirical Analysis with Special Reference to Education*, first published in 1964. Moreover, the concept of human capital can be traced much farther back to the economist Adam Smith (1723–1790) in *The Wealth of Nations* and to Alfred Marshall (1842–1924) in *Principles of Economics*.

Interestingly, Professor Becker made the following comments in the introduction to an early edition of his famous work: "It may seem odd now, but I hesitated a while before deciding to call my book *Human Capital*, and even hedged the risk by using a long subtitle. In the early days, many people were criticizing this term and the underlying analysis because they believed it treated people like slaves or machines." He went on to say, "My, how the world has changed! The name and analysis are now readily accepted by most people not only in the social sciences but even in the media."

An Appreciation That Grows with Age

Over the years, in addition to introducing my 20-year-old students to the holistic personal balance sheet, I have also presented this concept to older executives, MBA students, and general audiences made up of people in their 40s and 50s. Most were enthusiastic and accepting of this way of thinking about the value of human capital, although some were not. One objection I have heard, especially from those in traditional business accounting disciplines, is that human capital shouldn't be placed in the same category as financial capital— as (despite my fondness for the analogy) it isn't an oil well or gold mine that can be sold today for a known sum. These skeptics object to human capital—which is uncertain future earnings—being awarded a place on the personal balance sheet. After all, the critics claim that human capital can't be securitized, sold, or traded, so how can it be treated in the same way as tangible stocks and bonds?

To audiences who argue against the human capital and holistic personal balance sheet approaches—especially people in their middle working years—I pose a question in response, to wit: *How much of your financial capital would you be willing to give up, today, to turn back the clock a few decades and get back your old human capital?*

How much money would you be willing to pay, right now, to become 20 years younger? Most of it? All of it? Many, if not most of the skeptics say they would be willing to pay quite a lot indeed to regain some years of youth. Well, I reply, if you are willing to sacrifice so much financial capital at advanced ages to regain lost human capital, then it must be worth quite a bit at early ages!

The Nine Milestones

What does human capital have to do with financial milestones and financial decisions? Throughout your lifetime, as you reach what I am calling different "money milestones," to make good decisions you must understand the hidden assets and hidden liabilities on your holistic personal balance sheet. Going to school, getting married, having children, buying a home, buying insurance, filing your income tax each year, planning for retirement, making decisions about pensions—all of these milestones affect your holistic personal balance sheet.[8] The concept of human capital, as the largest and most valuable asset class for most people over most of their lifetimes, is probably the biggest single factor that you must, in my view, appreciate and include in your personal financial planning across your lifespan. Accordingly, this book takes human capital thinking and applies it to nine major financial milestones you can expect to grapple with in your life.

Now, I'll be the first to admit that the number 9—which appears both in the title of this book and is the number of chapter topics to follow—is both debatable and subjective. In fact, my perceptive wife claims I first plucked this number straight out of thin air and then labored to identify topics that added up to the said 9. And, although I won't admit to such extreme arbitrariness, I'm open to the argument that there might be only 7 or possibly as many as 12 important financial milestones over the course of your life. However, quibbling about whether there are more or less than 9 is not what this book is about.

---

8. In my previous book, *Are You a Stock or a Bond?* (also published by Pearson/FT Press, 2009), I addressed the narrow implications of human capital on investment portfolio management. In this book, I expand this thinking to all the major financial decisions in your life.

Truthfully, the nine topics I identified are far from homogenous in decision structure or actually even comparable to each other in economic magnitude. Some topics, such as marriage—which I examine in Chapter 4, ("Are Kids Investments and Can Marriages Diversity?")—have psychological and sociological dimensions that reach far beyond financial aspects. Furthermore, the typical marriage decision itself takes place once, twice, or maybe a handful of times over the course of the human life cycle (okay, two handfuls in the case of Elizabeth Taylor). In contrast, other decisions such as investment and portfolio management—which are reviewed in Chapter 8 ("Portfolio Construction: What Asset Class Do You Belong To?")—are primarily financial in nature and take place continuously in time. Can all of these milestones really be lumped together?

The purpose of highlighting these nine milestones is not to disregard or disrespect the nonfinancial elements in our lives and decisions *but rather to illuminate the often-obscured monetary implications*. The unavoidable truth is that children are expensive to raise and can place a strain on the family's finances; initially sound marriages can fail as a result of financial difficulties; and people can experience long periods of unemployment if they don't have proper career training—or if they overinvest in an education that doesn't increase the value of their human capital. In short, ignoring the monetary implications of our decisions can lead to financial regret.

Money Milestones over Your Lifetime

Whatever starting point you are coming from—whether you have already been converted to my way of thinking about human capital, or you plan to evaluate the concept as you move along—this book is designed to get you to think more broadly about your holistic balance sheet. I illustrate how the four basic principles of arithmetic—addition, subtraction, multiplication, and especially division—can be used as a guide for approaching all the money milestones in your life.

So far, I have talked about the value of human capital at specific points in time—such as my hypothetical physician's, engineer's, or baker's human capital value at the age of 25. However, another critical thing to understand about human capital is that it is *dynamic*—its value changes over time. (And it can also be changed by providing inputs such as higher education, as you shall see in Chapter 1, on investing in human capital through higher education.) And as you know from the examples I have provided to date, the value of your human capital generally decreases with age, as the number of years you intend to work decreases.

Accordingly, as you age, and your remaining human capital value declines, you should be converting or transforming your human capital into traditional financial capital by saving a fraction of your wages and income. This saving process is critical to meeting your money milestones effectively, and I address the question of "How much is enough?" in Chapter 2 ("What Is the Point of Saving Money Forever?").

Marriage and children can also have profound impacts on your holistic balance sheet, both positive and negative. I discuss the decision to marry and the decision to (and the cost to) have children in Chapter 4. Typically coincident with decisions about marriage and children are decisions about home ownership. You look at that issue in Chapter 6 ("Can You Eat Your House or Will It Ever Pay Dividends?"), along with the related topic of borrowing money in Chapter 3 ("How Much Debt Is Too Much and How Much Is Too Little?"). The value of human capital must also be protected, especially earlier in life—which is where life, disability, health, and critical illness insurance (all of which I discuss in Chapter 7, "Insurance Salesmen and Warranty Peddlers: Are They Smooth Enough?") come into play. As you save a fraction of your earnings, you need to make sure you pay as little tax as needed—to retain the maximum value—and this is a theme of Chapter 5 ("Government Tax Authorities: Partners, Adversaries, or Bazaar Merchants?").

Finally, as you near the end of your working years and arrive at what is traditionally referred to as retirement, the value of your human capital inevitably declines in value. At this stage, the bulk of the assets on your personal balance sheet should consist of the financial capital you have acquired. The conversion of your human capital to financial capital to sustain you in your nonworking years is, of course, the reason why retirement planning is so important. You cover this topic in Chapter 8 (on investing financial capital) and Chapter 9 (on creating income streams in retirement).

Summary: The Four Principles of Arithmetic in Action

- This book will use four basic principles to understand and evaluate your financial decisions through all the significant milestones in the human life cycle.

- To apply the four principles effectively, you need to ADD the true value of your financial capital and human capital together. That is your net worth.

- After you add your human capital to your holistic personal balance sheet, make sure to SUBTRACT all your liabilities to finally arrive at your economic resources.

- DIVIDE your total economic resources evenly and smoothly over your lifetime. MULTIPLY all the possible universes you might encounter in the future and act to smooth resources across all of them.

The four bullet points might not make much sense to you at this point, but I promise it will all click in a few chapters.

1

Is the Long-Term Value of an Education Worth the Short-Term Cost?

One of my rather bright undergraduate students from a few years ago, who stayed in touch over the years, decided after some years in the labor force to invest (more) in her human capital by returning to graduate school. She wanted to get a master's degree in advanced mathematical finance. I encouraged her to look broadly and consider all the top schools around the world. After a grueling application and admissions process, she was finally accepted to one of the best graduate schools, which happens to be located in the U.S. Midwest. This was quite an achievement for her, and I suspect her acceptance letter has been framed for posterity.

Unfortunately, a few weeks after the good news came in the mail, she got a follow-up letter from the school with the financial details and a huge invoice. She was facing a total cost of almost $80,000 for a graduate education that takes less than two years to complete. (She probably didn't want to frame the invoice.) And although she understood that this was a great investment in her human capital, at the same time, she didn't have $80,000 sitting in a bank account ready to be withdrawn. Furthermore, this was a full-time, intense program that would limit her ability to earn any outside labor income while she was in school. So, like most prospective students, she began investigating various private loans through banks and organizations such as Sallie Mae and government-run student loan programs such as the Federal Direct Loan Program. The paperwork was daunting, the money wasn't free, and she started having some doubts. Was $80,000 in additional debt really worth it? After all, she was still paying off some of her undergraduate student loans.

Investing in a Gold Mine...Called Anastasia

When I found out about the dilemma she was facing—and the possibility she might abandon her educational plans—I offered Anastasia *(not her real name, obviously)* a deal, which I will outline here. I knew she was a bright and hard-working student who would do extremely well in graduate school and complete the program in the top of her class. My estimate was that she would then go on to a successful career in the financial services industry and likely earn thousands of dollars a year in salary and bonus. In my view, she had the potential of a high-producing gold mine or oil well, and I personally wanted the opportunity to invest in her human capital. So, I offered her $50,000 in cash—to finance the majority of her tuition—in exchange for a mere 10 percent of her pretax earnings during the first ten years after she graduated. To my way of thinking, the money I offered wasn't a loan or any type of debt. It was an investment. As long as she was in school, and wasn't earning any money, she owed nothing. I invited her to think of this as accepting a slightly higher tax rate in the future in exchange for a deeply subsidized education today.

Should We Allow Human Capital Derivatives?

As you saw in the Introduction, "Human Capital: Your Greatest Asset," investing time and money to develop your human capital pays off on average. But the dividends and investment returns—especially given student loan interest payments—might be less than in previous years, as the cost of investing in human capital (getting a college degree) continues to increase faster than inflation (as measured by the consumer price index, or CPI).[1] This is especially true for elite private colleges and universities, in which tuition has risen the most and the fastest. College graduates in aggregate have more student loan debt than ever before and are entering the labor force with

---

1. University tuition fees have risen faster than inflation over the past decade in both Canada and the United States. For U.S. data, see Baum and Ma, *Trends in College Pricing.* Canadian data taken from Statistics Canada, "The Daily: University Tuition Fees."

thousands of dollars in balance sheet liabilities, well before they have taken out their first mortgages.

According to an article in the *Wall Street Journal* on September 3, 2009, today, almost two thirds of all college students have borrowed money to pay for their tuition; their debt load upon graduation is an average of slightly more than $23,000.

Is there an alternative? I think so.

Here's what I'm thinking: Perhaps there will come a day in the not-too-distant future when current and future students can sell a fraction of their (extraordinarily valuable) human capital when they are young to finance the costs of investing in education and going to school. These young students would get a lump sum of cash in advance or, alternatively, spread out over their years in school. These sums would not be considered a loan, or "bond-like." Rather, the funds would be considered "stock-like"—that is, similar to a company or a small business issuing shares (via an IPO or seasoned equity offering) to finance its expansion and investment opportunities. The money would be repaid by the student, eventually, in the form of pre-ferred dividends for a predetermined period starting after gradua-tion. I'm calling this concept *Human Capital DerivativeS* (HuCaDS), or, with tongue in cheek, *Human Capital Daddy of Sugar.*

Here's how I figured the math. When Anastasia graduated in approximately 24 months, I anticipated she would be earning at least six digits—given her previous experience and the typical salary struc-ture for specialists in her field. And, even if her salary remained con-stant at $100,000 per year (pretax) for the next ten years, that would yield me $10,000 for ten years on an initial investment of $50,000. To analyze this more precisely, I calculated something called the internal rate of return (or IRR) in my Excel spreadsheet program. A cash out-flow of 50,000 today followed by zero cash flows for two years (while she is in school) and then by a positive cash flow of $10,000 from years 2 through 12 represents an annualized return of 10.25 percent. That investment return is much better than the rates at my local bank.

In fact, this deal could turn out even better for both of us. Let's imagine that Anastasia performs better than expected, and by her fifth year back in the labor force, she is earning $200,000 per year. So, for the first five years I would receive $10,000 in dividends and for the remaining five years of our HuCaDS agreement, she would be sending me $20,000 each year to pay back my investment. That works out to an internal rate of return—for me—of 15.2%. This is better than you can hope for even in the most irrational of stock market bubbles!

Of course, my HuCaDS arrangement would also leave me exposed to some downside risk as well. Anastasia might decide to shelve her completed master's degree and backpack across Europe or India for five years after graduation, which might satisfy her lifetime ambition to travel the world but would generate zero dividends for me. In that case, her return to the labor force would leave me only five years of cash flows in the contract term. Alternatively, she might decide to join the U.S. Peace Corps—or take a minimum-wage job at McDonalds paying only $25,000. Then the internal rate of return from my $50,000 investment would be zero, or possibly even negative. In those cases, I would have been better off putting the $50,000 under my mattress than investing in a HuCaDS with Anastasia. That is the risk and return trade-off for me: On the upside, I can get returns in the double digits—and on the downside, I could lose it all. Now I obviously would invest only a small fraction of my total net worth in human capital derivative arrangements, but at the same time, I would also derive some psychic dividends from having helped finance a student's education.

I mention this (true) story because I think it could serve as an alternative for future students to onerous and anonymous student loan debt, with potentially crushing interest payments. In my teaching career, I see firsthand how current levels of student loan debt force people into jobs and careers they don't want or like, simply because they have to make the loan payments. My HuCaDS proposal would enable graduates to accept any job they truly want, knowing that they owe only a floating fraction of their salary as opposed to a fixed and unyielding obligation, as with a student loan.

Securitizing Human Capital

Now, I am not the first person to think about securitizing human capital. (Securitization is the process by which a cash-flow-producing asset is repackaged as a security and sold to investors.) This concept can be traced back to the well-known economist Milton Friedman in an article titled, oddly enough, "The Role of Government in Education."[2] This concept has also more recently been advocated by Miguel Lleras in his book *Investing in Human Capital*. Friedman, Lleras, and others have pointed out some of the potential pitfalls in programs that attempt to securitize human capital. For example, how do you enforce payment? What happens in the event of a student's bankruptcy? Can these payments be considered tax-deductible from income, like corporate debt? Does such an arrangement risk being labeled usurious (that is, charging exorbitant amounts of interest) if income payments far exceed the initial equity investment? As with any ambitious plan, the details have to be ironed out. But I think the idea itself has merit and should be considered, at least on the individual level.

In the next few sections you will see how the decisions about where to go to school, how much time to spend learning, and what to study can together have a huge impact on the valuation of your human capital. Here's what I mean in practical terms: Two 25-year-old graduate students sharing an apartment might both have little in the way of financial capital, real liquid assets, or income. Their traditional accounting balance sheets likely display a negative net worth. Yet, depending on their chosen courses of study, their holistic balance sheets can look *completely different*. One might have a human capital worth millions of dollars, whereas for the other it might be measured in hundreds of thousands or even less. Moreover, as you will see from the discussion of the net worth and financial and asset holdings of college graduates, not only might their earning power be different, but the types of assets they are likely to hold in the future can also be quite different, which has yet other implications I explore in later chapters. Because I thought you might like to calculate the impact of an investment in human capital on your personal balance sheet, I have created a calculator at www.qwema.ca that enables you to project the payoff from an investment in human capital, based on your age, expected investment in education, and expected increase in income.

---

2. In Robert A. Solo, ed., *Economics and the Public Interest*.

In short: Education decisions have deep and persistent impacts on your financial situation for the rest of your life span, and those impacts are not necessarily obvious at the outset of your educational path. The undergraduates I encounter in my personal finance course have already made the decision to attend college, and they've already (for the most part) chosen their course of study. This chapter is designed to get my thinking about the impact of education on human capital into the hands of a bigger audience—so you or your kids, too, can properly estimate and add the value of investing in human capital to your personal balance sheet.

Using the metaphor of Dynamic Control Theory (DCT), education is one of the variables that impacts your financial well-being and that is controllable. (You can control how much you get!) In a life filled with uncertainty, there is robust evidence that educational attainments pay off over time, and that they can set you up to achieve far greater wealth than you might otherwise.

Are College Graduates Truly Wealthier?

In the introduction, I mentioned that I ask the undergraduate students in my personal finance course two questions. The first (optimistic) question is whether they think their personal balance sheet will look better in ten years' time than it does now. The second, seemingly more pessimistic, question asks whether their present net worth is zero or even negative. The introduction to this book is largely focused on uncovering the true, but hidden, answer to that second question. As you now know, invariably, when their human capital is included, my students are wealthier than they first thought—as are you.

But if you accept the concept of human capital as the most valuable asset class on your personal balance sheet for most of your working life, you also must accept that this is a resource that is depleted over time. That is: The flip side, or corollary, of the optimistic "You are wealthier than you think" message is that if you don't save an appropriate proportion of this wealth—that is, the dividends you reap from your human capital—then you might find your total personal balance sheet to be in *worse*, not better, shape as you age. Remember, with each passing year you have one less year of proven reserves to draw on (returning to our oil-well metaphor). Furthermore, if you take on a disproportionate amount of student loan—or other—debt relative to the income you can expect from your chosen career, your holistic balance sheet might actually shrink over time. Accordingly, decisions about education do not just influence us at the point they are made but can affect the value of our human capital for the remainder of our lives. Indeed, education decisions are some of the most important milestones you will face in life.

So, let's take a closer look at the income, net worth, and personal debts of college graduates and compare them to high school graduates, all to get a better sense of how the education decisions you make impact your human capital. We'll conclude with some suggestions about how best to finance college education, the increasingly expensive investment in human capital.

The Best-Paying Careers?

For many previous generations, and in the eyes of many economists until about a half-century ago, paying for higher education was not considered an investment but rather a consumption good such as an expensive suit, car, or set of golf clubs: It might make you feel better about yourself but didn't necessarily have an investment value. Today most people would agree that financial returns to education can be quite substantial. That is, money spent on college education is generally perceived much more like an investment that will pay dividends well into the future. According to estimates by the International Monetary Fund and the World Bank, the private return to education—what the individual college student can expect to gain— is between 20 percent and 30 percent and the social return—or what society gains from investments in post-secondary education—is from 10 percent to 20 percent.[3] The lesson is clear: Investing in human capital pays dividends. But the question of how much is paid out depends significantly on your choices about post-secondary education. How so?

According to a May 2009 cover story in *U.S. News and World Report*, the median national pay for a hairstylist is $33,700 per year.

---

3. As reported in Lleras, *Investing in Human Capital*.

In contrast, an optometrist earns a median $99,700, which is three times as much as the hairstylist.[4] According to the story, the employment outlook for both professions is good, and despite the pay gap, both groups report high job satisfaction. Now, guess which one of these two professions requires more effort, education, and training? Yes, the optometrist. You can probably work as a successful hairstylist with barely a high school diploma (or less) and a short training period. In contrast, to become an optometrist requires an O.D. degree, which means, in turn, that you need to spend four years and beyond in college.

The gap between the expected incomes of a hairstylist and an optometrist, and between the years of study required for each profession, provides an important lesson in the economics of the development of human capital. Unlike most forms of financial capital, you can't actually inherit human capital, win it in the lottery, or stumble across it in an antique sale. Most people have to work hard and invest time and effort in nurturing their human capital. In general, the more you are willing to invest in human capital—in terms of time, money, and effort—the greater the financial payoff. More important, when you "mark-to-market" the holistic balance sheet of two 25-year-olds, one studying to be a hairstylist and the other an optometrist, the human capital value of the optometrist is more than three times as great as that of the hairstylist. I estimate that the optometrist's human capital is worth approximately $1.8 million whereas the hairstylist's is worth $0.6 million.[5]

Minor Initial Differences Magnify over Time

As you can see, even a small difference in annual wage income can lead to enormous differences in the holistic balance sheet over time. This point was emphasized in a study of college majors discussed

---

4. Using Canadian data from Payscale.com, median salaries are estimated at $99,300 for an optometrist and $26,000 for a hairstylist in Canada.

5. Using Canadian data from Payscale.com and QWeMA Group calculations, I estimate a Canadian optometrist's human capital value at $2.1 million, compared to $0.5 million for a hairstylist in Canada.

in a recent issue of *Forbes* magazine.[6] According to data from the website PayScale.com and published in *Forbes*, a college graduate who majored in English and had less than five years of experience earned a median wage slightly less than $40,000 in 2008. An English major with 10 years to 20 years of experience earned approximately $60,000 per year. Thus, roughly speaking, the premium for experience was $20,000 per year.

In contrast, according to the same survey, a mechanical engineering college grad with less than five years of experience earned a median $60,000 in 2008, which is approximately $20,000 more per year than the English major. Furthermore, the mechanical engineer with 10 years to 20 years of experience earned a median $90,000 in wages. The experience premium in this case is $30,000 per year.

Thus, I would argue that the human capital of a mechanical engineer who is just about to graduate is (much) more valuable than the human capital of an English major for two reasons: First, the engineer's initial wage out of college is greater than the English major's, and secondly, the premium she will be paid for the experience she builds over time is higher as well. Thus, the present value of the after-tax wages for the two graduates over the estimated 40 years of income is greater. For the English major I estimate it is $1 million and for the mechanical engineer it is $1.5 million. (Now, wouldn't it be useful to know this as you contemplate college majors?) Stay tuned for more insights into how education decisions affect wealth-building over time.

How Investing in Human Capital Pays

One of the common questions I get from eager young students who drop by my office is what they should major in or study at school. Some pose this as an existential, big-picture question: "What should I do with my life?" Others phrase it as a more targeted question: "I want to work in the investment industry. So, am I better off taking advanced managerial accounting or advanced derivative pricing?"

---

6. Badenhausen, "The Most Lucrative College Majors."

Despite what I've already said about varying pay scales by profession, and keeping in mind I am most definitely not a guidance counselor, my answer is usually as follows: First, figure out what you truly enjoy doing. A good way to do this is by taking as many different courses as possible. Then, when you find what you like, find out how to make money doing that. Although the answer might not satisfy them, this little piece of advice was given to me by my father many years ago, and it has worked out well for me personally. Although I've just spent the last few pages talking about the financial impacts of education decisions, the bottom line, for me, is that human capital estimates should form only part of your decision about what career to pursue. (However, I do think they should form at least part of your deliberations.) Somebody who truly wants to be a hairstylist but who decides to pursue a career as an optometrist because it pays three times as much will likely have a higher human capital value than they otherwise would—but they are also much more likely to be miserable!

I'm sure these remarks will sound odd if you worry about your kids who just love playing video games...or sleeping all day. Surely figuring out what you enjoy is not the best strategy for increasing the value of human capital, is it? Shouldn't professors be telling students to "aim high" and go to medical school or become engineers or lawyers?

Oddly enough, additional research—beyond what I've already reported—provides some subtle reasons for the discrepancy between the net worth of people with and without higher education. That is, the gap in net worth between people with a college degree and those with a high school diploma or less is attributable to more than just educational achievement. How so? Let's explore this question next.

First, let's start by examining actual household balance sheet values as estimated and reported by the U.S. Federal Reserve, as opposed to the theoretical estimates I have been giving for human capital (see Table 1.1).

Here are some basic facts. According to 2007 data collected by the U.S. Federal Reserve in its Survey of Consumer Finances,[7] the

---

7. The SCF is a triennial interview survey of U.S. families sponsored by the Board of Governors of the Federal Reserve System with cooperation of the U.S. Department of the Treasury. In the year 2007 survey, 4,422 families were interviewed. See Bucks et al, "Changes in U.S. Family Finances from 2004 to 2007" for more information.

TABLE 1.1   Does Education Pay Dividends?: Federal Reserve Board Survey of Consumer Finances 2007

Education Level (Head of Household)	Percent of U.S. Population in Group	Average Pretax Household Income	Average Household Net Worth	Median Household Net Worth
No High School Diploma	13.5%	$31,300	$142,900	$33,000
High School Diploma	32.9%	$51,100	$251,600	$80,300
Some College	18.4%	$68,100	$365,900	$84,700
College Degree	35.3%	$143,800	$1,097,800	$280,800

average net worth of U.S. college graduates is much larger than the net worth of individuals who don't have a high school diploma, or who didn't attend college. For example, in the year 2007, the average net worth of a family in which the head of the household has a high-school diploma only—and did not go on to college—was $251,600, whereas the average net worth for a college graduate was almost four times greater at roughly one million dollars. For those without a high school diploma, the average net worth was a mere $142,900.[8] (Note that all these numbers use the conventional accounting measures of net worth—namely explicit financial assets minus explicit financial liabilities—and don't take into account the human capital value I previously discussed.)

Human Capital Investments over Time

No matter how you report the statistics, one thing is quite clear from the data: A college education—which is an investment in human capital—is statistically associated with greater net worth and greater

---

8. These patterns are seen in Canada as well. Median net worth for households with less than a high school diploma was $92,433 in 2005; with a high school diploma was $120,007; and with a university degree was $237,400. From Statistics Canada, *The Wealth of Canadians*.

Detour: Averages Versus Medians

Before you go any further, I want to take a minute to review the difference between *averages* and *medians*. (If this distinction is already familiar to you, skip ahead.) Note that the numbers you've been reviewing on net worth are simple averages (also known as the *statistical mean*). Averages can be distorted by large values (for example, Bill Gates or Warren Buffet pulling the average earnings up). Another measure of the middle or expected value of a data set is the *median*. The median net worth is more robust than the average (that is, not as sensitive to outliers such as Buffet or Gates) because it identifies the point at which 50 percent of the population has a net worth above these numbers and 50 percent are below. Just to be sure this distinction is clear, think of the series of numbers: 2,10,9,2,4,7,1,1,3,7. If you add them up and divide by 10, you arrive at a mean or average value of 4.6. On the other hand, if you rank them from highest to lowest, the mid-point, or median value, will be between 3 and 4. In general, for the same group of numbers, the *average* and the *median* can be quite different. If, for example, the numbers I've just given represented average and median earnings of a group of people, the difference would be quite large.

income. As you can see from Table 1.1, the household headed by a college graduate had an average income of $143,800 in the year 2007 versus $51,100 for those who completed high school—and just $31,300 for those without a high school diploma.[9] (One of the first economists to demonstrate this was Columbia University professor Jacob Mincer in his 1974 book *Schooling, Experience and Earnings*.)

As you might suspect, these multiples were not just limited to the year 2007. The gap is consistent across time. Eighteen years earlier, in

---

9. This finding holds true in Canada, as well: average earnings for those with less than a high school diploma were $21,230 in 2001; those with a high school diploma earned $25,477 annually; and those with a university degree earned $48,648 annually. From 2001 census data as reported in Statistics Canada, *Earnings of Canadians*.

1989, the average net worth of college graduates was $672,400 whereas the equivalent number for high school graduates was $200,900. Notice that over that 18-year period the average net worth of college graduates increased by almost 63 percent—from a value of $672,400 to $1,097,800—whereas the average net worth of high school graduates increased by only 25 percent. (These amounts are all given in 2007 dollars, which means they are already inflation-adjusted. That is, the gap is not a function of inflation.) Indeed, this appears to provide yet more evidence of the long-term benefit that accrues from investing in human capital: Your net worth is both higher and increases faster. However, the reasons are more subtle than you think.

College Grads Learn to Buy Different Assets

It seems that U.S. college graduates are wealthier partly because they own different types of physical assets and financial investments. And it is these underlying components of net worth—which are quite oblivious to the education level of their owner—which have increased in value, which leads to an increase in net worth. For example, according to the same Survey of Consumer Finances data you previously saw, in the year 2007 more than 31 percent of college graduates owned stocks (directly), and 21 percent held investment funds. In contrast, only 9 percent of those with a high school diploma reported holding any stocks (directly), and only 6 percent had any investment funds.

A similar pattern emerges with nonfinancial assets such as real estate. For example, in the same 2007 survey, 78 percent of college graduates reported owning a primary residence, whereas only 53 percent of individuals without a high school diploma owned a primary residence. For high school graduates the ownership rate was 69 percent. Even more noteworthy is the median value of the houses owned by the various educational groups: The median value of the college graduate's primary residence was $280,000. For the high school graduate it was $150,000, and for those without a high school diploma it was $122,500.

What you can see is that the college graduate's higher net worth is allocated to a portfolio of assets that are quite different from those in the other groups who have less education. In aggregate, college graduates have more financial investments, and they own houses that are more expensive. Now, think about what happened to the value of the stock market, mutual funds, and housing prices during the period 1989 to 2007; they went up quite strongly. The SP500 increased by 659 percent from January 1989 to January 2007, whereas the value of housing—as measured by the S&P/Case-Shiller Home Price (Composite 10) index, which provides data on single-family house prices in the United States—increased by 187 percent over the same 18 years.

So, perhaps the reason college graduates are wealthier than high school graduates is because of what they "learned to buy" while in college, as opposed to their earning power *per se*. In the words of the author of a recent study on the same topic, "Assets more likely held by college graduates appreciate faster than assets held by high school graduates."[10] This insight is also echoed in a Harvard Business School working paper in which the authors examine the impact of financial education on financial market participation and find that cognitive ability, which is arguably improved by attending college, increases the odds of holding financial assets such as stocks and bonds.[11] Of course, these same assets can become a double-edged sword because they are more volatile than other kinds of assets, and this volatility is not under their individual owner's control.

What you've seen so far is that households headed by individuals with more education tend to have higher incomes and higher net worth. The higher net worth comes in part because college graduates hold different assets than those owned by households with lower levels of education, and these components of net worth appreciate more quickly. But you also know that the assets held by households with higher education levels fluctuate in value more than those held by other households. Does this mean that college graduates might become worse off, over time, than other households with less education?

---

10. Yamashita, "Keeping up with the Joneses in McMansions."
11. Cole and Shastry, "Smart Money."

Could the Fortunes of College Graduates Wane?

Let's take a closer look at the Survey of Consumer Finances (SCF) numbers on household assets. We'll focus on two groups: the college graduate household (which represents 35 percent of the U.S. population) and the high school graduate household (which represents 33 percent of the U.S. population).

Recall that college graduates are more likely to be homeowners, and the value of their principal residence is higher as well. The college graduate owns a home with a median value of $280,000 whereas the homes owned by high school graduate households have a median value of $150,000. (All these are 2007 numbers, which is well before the housing mini-crash of the last few years.) More important, let's examine the debt and mortgages college and high school graduates have on those houses.

According to the SCF data, 62 percent of college graduates report having a mortgage secured by their primary residence, versus 45 percent of the high school graduate group. In addition, the college graduate has median debts of $124,000 versus only $40,000 in debt for the high school graduate group. The college graduate has more than three times as much debt as the high school graduate, including mortgages, installment loans, credit card debt, and other unsecured lines of credit. So, although the college graduate net worth is much higher than the high school graduate, their (traditional) balance sheet looks different as well. They have both *more assets* and *more debt*. Moreover, the assets they own are more susceptible to fluctuations in the market prices of real estate and stock markets.

So, will the college graduates be (that much) better off in the future? Or might the increased volatility of their financial and real estate holdings potentially pull their net worth down? Or perhaps the relatively safe investment in education enables college graduates to take more investment risk with their traditional financial capital—because they're invested more heavily in an asset class (human capital) that stands to pay dividends over a long period of time, they are set up to assume more risk with the rest of their (financial) assets. Right now, the questions I'm posing have no firm answers. My intention here is to illuminate some of the surprising financial impacts of a college education—impacts that I think are worth considering when contemplating education decisions. The rest of this book guides you through protecting your wealth as you move through money milestones, including how to assess and adjust the amount of financial risk you take on.

The SCF includes some other interesting statistics about the value of human capital. It turns out that people who are classified as self-employed, as opposed to working for someone else, report both greater income and much greater net worth. In 2007 the self-employed household reported an average net worth of almost $2,000,000 compared to only $350,000 for those who work for others. This means that Americans who are their own bosses are six times wealthier in conventional net worth terms than those who are employees—and they may be happier, as well, given their increased work autonomy. It is likely that one of the reasons for this discrepancy in net worth is that the mean reported household income for the self-employed is more than double that of those who work for others: $191,000 versus $83,100.

Does the Ivy League Pay Greater Dividends?

So, now that you know that higher education pays dividends, you might wonder whether the particular kind of college education you get makes a difference to how much you can earn over your lifetime. Is there a premium for an Ivy League education?

When my eldest daughter was born, more than 15 years ago, the first word I wanted her to learn—before the conventional *mommy* or *daddy* or *bottle*—was Harvard. I would buy her cute little shirts with Harvard logos; sweatshirts with Harvard emblazoned on the front; Harvard cups, mugs, key chains, and more. Then, when she was no more than seven or eight years of age I took her with me on a business trip to Boston and we visited the campus. (It was freezing and pouring rain all day. She hated it.) As you can tell, I was *just a little obsessed* with the idea that she should go to Harvard.

As my other children were born—I have four daughters in total—I taught them the words *Yale, Stanford*, and *Princeton*, in that order. In my mind, they were destined for the Ivy League with all the rewards and benefits this education brings.

Then I got real.

The cost of one year's (undergraduate) tuition at Harvard is now $33,700. At Yale, the number is $35,300. These numbers are not anomalies: The average cost of tuition at a private university (in the United States) is approximately $25,000 per year. And these amounts don't include another $15,000 or so in annual living expenses and other fees. In contrast, the average cost of state university tuition is a mere $6,600 per year. Now compare these costs (five to seven times more for Ivy League versus state college) to data published by Payscale.com, which indicate that the median starting salary for an Ivy League college graduate ranges from $56,200 to $66,500. This not much more—between about 7 percent and 21 percent more—than the median starting salary of $52,400 reported for the top state schools. At first glance, you might wonder if an Ivy League education is worthwhile. If you pay five to seven times more for tuition at an elite private college, shouldn't you earn five to seven times more right out of the gate?

However, research does tend to support the notion that it pays off (literally), over time, to attend an elite private college. In a report published by the National Bureau of Economic Research in the United States, the authors examined this specific question.[12] Analyzing the payoff of attending Ivy League and other colleges is not as easy as you might think. Clearly, some graduates from Harvard and Yale are unemployed (or volunteering at the Peace Corps), and some graduates from the lowest-ranked state schools make millions of dollars playing professional basketball or football. Accordingly, studies of the earnings over time of graduates from Ivy League and state colleges focus on averages and medians.

How do these studies measure the quality of schools, and how do they measure the earnings of students from different schools over time? First, to gauge the relative quality of different colleges, our

---

12. Brewer, Eide, and Ehrenberg, "Does it Pay to Attend an Elite Private College?"

researchers used library budgets, the SAT scores of entering freshman, and the number of faculty per student. (Generous library budgets, high SAT scores, and lots of faculty per student drove the rankings up.)

Then, to investigate the earnings over time from graduates of different colleges in the United States, the researchers used results from the NLS 1972 dataset, which is conducted by the National Center for Education Statistics. This data contains detailed family and schooling characteristics for various cohorts of students: 21,000 students who graduated high school in 1972 and an additional more than 10,000 who graduated in 1980 and 1982. These groups were interviewed 6, 10, and 14 years after they completed high school, so the researchers extracted quite a bit of information on the relation between college quality and earnings, among a number of other variables.

Their results were conclusive and robust. The researchers concluded "There is a large premium to attending an elite private institution and a smaller premium to attending a middle-rated private institution, relative to a bottom-rated public school." They also noted that their analyses suggest the return to elite private colleges "increased significantly for the 1980s cohort compared to the 1970s cohort." As this research was conducted more than ten years ago, it will be interesting to see if a trend develops, and the 1990s cohort—people graduating from high school in the 1990s—does even better than the 1980s cohort does.

Yet, despite all the positive evidence, the authors were careful to end their study by saying: "We do not attempt to determine the cause of this change, but it is a potentially important finding in light of the large tuition increases concentrated at these institutions during the past two decades." In other words, although the authors could not pinpoint the specific reasons for the "large premium" accruing to graduates of elite private colleges relative to graduates of middle- and bottom-ranked schools, they suggest the high tuition and significant tuition increases at elite schools might be offset by later financial gains to the graduates of these schools. Keep in mind, too, it is not just the earnings and wages that are higher for (elite) college graduates—as you have explored, their personal balance sheets look quite different as well.

Distinct Groups of Students—And "Fun Capital"

Either way, it does seem that to afford tuition—whether at expensive private schools or not—students are incurring a substantial and increasing amount of debt. The average amount of debt held by a typical undergraduate rose from $16,000 in the early 1990s to $20,100 in 2007 (all reported in constant 2007 dollars). Just recently the *Wall Street Journal* reported that it has reached $23,000 in 2009.[13] Although these numbers might seem relatively low to those earning many times that amount in one year of work, I know from my own years teaching at a university that some students are taking on much more than this average amount of debt to make it through with a degree—and the bulk of students do take out loans to finance their education. According to the Annual Survey of Colleges, approximately 60 percent of undergraduate students graduate with some student loan debt and this number might be as high as 70 percent for 2010.[14]

But what of the 40 percent with no debt? Perhaps some students have (wealthy) parents and grandparents who saved for their children's education and have thus contributed the bulk of the cost. Yet other diligent students manage to find the time to work at one (or two or three) part-time jobs, the earnings from which enable them to avoid any debt or loans. I have tremendous respect and great sympathy for these kids—and they are kids—who have to endure a full semester-load of coursework in addition to an additional 20 to 30 hours of paid work per week. These students rarely have time for anything else, and I make a habit to remind them to keep track of all the debt they do *not* incur, compared to their peers with student loans. With no debt, their holistic net worth is greater, and their holistic balance sheet will likely look much better in five to ten years. In my view, this *lack of debt* should be valued and quantified.

---

13. See Baum and Payea, *Trends in Student Aid*.
14. See Baum and Payea, *Trends in Student Aid*. In Canada 54 percent of students with a bachelor's degree graduate with debt. From Bayard and Greenlee, *Graduating in Canada*.

I would even argue that indebted students, who have decided to finance their education by borrowing, should really keep track of all the time they spent having fun while in college, using a journal or keeping a running total. When these graduates come to me with concerns about all the debt they have incurred and now have to repay, I remind them of their colleagues who likely spent much less time at parties and bars, and hence avoided debt. These students should perhaps create another asset class on the left side of the holistic balance sheet called "fun capital" to record the sum total of all the hours they spent clubbing while investing in their human capital.

Did Anastasia Accept the Offer?

By the way, in case you were wondering, Anastasia, the student who was trying to figure out how to finance her education, turned down my offer for an equity stake in her future labor income. She protested that it felt too much like slavery. In fact, she is not alone in feeling that way. Despite being an advocate for the idea, this is what none other than Professor Friedman wrote about human capital contracts back in his 1962 classic *Capitalism and Freedom*: "...they are economically equivalent to the purchase of a share in an individual's earning capacity, and thus partial to slavery." I guess even he had his doubts. Oh well. Perhaps I personally shouldn't have been so greedy. Maybe next time I'll ask for 5 percent dividends instead of 10 percent.

Summary: The Four Principles in Action

- Investing in education can clearly ADD to the value of your human capital, although you might incur debt that you must SUBTRACT from your holistic balance sheet. The equation only makes sense if the difference between the additional human capital value and the debt is positive.

- The premium you can command from higher education will be MULTIPLIED over your entire working life, so be careful not to think myopically about the benefits over short versus long periods of time.

- Remember that the total gains to you can be DIVIDED to raise your standard of living every year through your entire life span. More on this in later chapters.

2

What Is the Point of Saving Money Forever?

As you might expect, my business students are required to complete a number of finance-related courses and topics to obtain their degrees. The most significant among them by far is our corporate finance course, in which they learn the foundations of managing the finances of a corporation. In this course, they are taught early on that the objective of the modern corporation is to *maximize shareholder value*. We tell them that all a corporation's activities—its dividend policy, compensation practices, and even the amount of money it borrows—should be geared toward creating the most value for individual shareholders.

This maximize shareholder value (or MSV) mantra is also emphasized in many of the other business courses they take. However, it has recently come under some intellectual pressure as commentators have questioned whether interests other than those of shareholders, such as value to the company's employees, the community in which the company is located, or even the broader physical environment, should be considered and perhaps even take precedence. Nevertheless, MSV is still very much at the core of what is taught in business school. And the simplicity of this mantra has the benefit of helping young and eager students, who have little actual business experience, solve case studies and analyze complex business situations using the equivalent of high-school physics equations. To solve the case, just plug in the MSV formula.

So, when the professor asks the question: *Should the billion dollar company buy the million dollar supplier?* the 19-year-old junior answers, *yes*, claiming this move would maximize shareholder value.

Alternatively, when the homework queries whether the company should increase pension benefits to retirees, the ready answer is "no" from our 20-year-old senior: This option doesn't provide any additional value to shareholders.

When these students arrive in my personal finance course, which in contrast to corporate finance, deals with the individual as opposed to corporations, I start them off with the following question: What is the objective of the personal corporation I lightheartedly refer to as YOU, Inc.? Is there a test equivalent to MSV that can weigh different proposed courses of action when individual, not corporate, fortunes are at stake?

The students usually have a number of interesting and rather clever answers to this question. The most overtly ambitious and vocal ones tend to argue that the objective of YOU, Inc., is to make as much money as possible—legally, of course. I don't necessarily disagree with this answer but tell them it isn't much use as a guiding principle for milestone decisions about whether to buy or rent a house, or whether to get term or whole life insurance, or whether to invest in stocks or in bonds.

Other students answer that perhaps saving 10 percent of salary is the main operating objective. Another group suggests that retiring from work as young as possible is the goal to reach. Still others offer that the objective of YOU, Inc., is to maximize the value of human capital. (At least somebody was paying attention on the first day of class!) A select few advocate following spiritual paths or maximizing general feelings of happiness. For the most part, though, my experience is that the class doesn't reach consensus on the matter. At some point, they turn to me and announce, "Ok, Prof. We give up. What is *the* main objective that will guide us in weighing options for YOU, Inc.?" My answer? *Long Division*—you know, the standard procedure you all learned in grade school for dividing large numbers using a series of simple steps. But how can long division help us in making financial decisions? The rest of this chapter is devoted to explaining this simple and powerful insight.

The 25-to-25 Jackpot: What Would You Do?

Imagine the following situation: You are 25 years old and your long-lost and rather eccentric uncle, whom you rarely met and barely know, has just passed away. When the lawyers vet his will, they discover he left you $25 million dollars as an inheritance. Unbeknown to your family, he was quite wealthy—and it seems he took a liking to you personally. However, your money has been placed in an ironclad trust, which you can't access for the next 25 years. (Let's assume that even the best lawyers in town cannot break or dissolve the trust agreement.) It appears your uncle was concerned about your financial maturity, and he decided it would be best to wait until you are (much) older before giving you title to this unprecedented sum of cash. So, the money is inaccessible for the next quarter century—and in exactly 25 years, the trustees will hand you a check for $25 million dollars.

My question to you is: What do you do in the meantime? Let's say you have little, if any, financial capital right now. Do you live like a pauper until the age of 50, waiting for the trust to become unlocked? Or do you spend recklessly—maybe even close to the entire $25 million—counting on your windfall to bail you out in 25 years?

Now, you don't really need to imagine an eccentric rich uncle and a surprise inheritance to get your imagination going. Instead, you could think of a peculiar lottery in which you have just won $25 million dollars but must wait 25 years to collect. Or perhaps you've accepted a job in which—with much suspension of disbelief—you must wait 25 years before you get $25 million in wages and bonus. I invite you to spend a few minutes thinking about this.

As you might have guessed, I pose this "25-to-25" thought experiment (25 years to 25 million, that is) to my undergraduate finance students in their personal finance course. What would they do? One of the first questions I get in response is: "Can you borrow against the money?" I tell them they can and, to make life easier, I ask them to assume interest rates for borrowing and lending are close to zero (which is pretty much what they are today, anyway). After we've established that borrowing against the lump sum is possible, my question to my students is, "How much of this $25 million would you borrow, exactly, and how would you spread your withdrawals over time?"

The answers called out in response are all over the map. Some students want to borrow against half the funds today, whereas others want to borrow against the entire amount. A minority few argue it would be best to wait and live within current means today and then "live it up" when the money is unlocked at age 50. Others respond that it's silly to live an impoverished life for 25 years and only enjoy wealth in the later part of life.

Discussion then turns to the question of what happens after you get access to the $25 million in trust. Do you spend it all then? Do you divide the funds into yearly allotments based on how long you expect to live and spend it year by year? The exchange is vigorous and interesting. Occasionally, when I have the time, I have the students form small groups and ask them to reach agreement about the best spending plan. I tell them to ignore complications such as premature death or ill health and assume they all will live to 75 years or 25 years past the unlocking of the locked trust.

Guiding Principle: Smoothing Consumption

Finally, after much back and forth, typically a consensus emerges from the small groups. The students announce they will definitely borrow against the $25 million. They will try not to borrow too much, so they do not risk depleting the pot, but at the same time they won't borrow too little and deprive themselves early in life. The class generally proposes the following solution: Borrow $500,000 each year for the next 25 years. After 25 years, they will have spent exactly $12.5 million, or half the total allotment. This leaves another $12.5 million to last for the remaining 25 years—with $500,000 available to spend each year from ages 25 to 75. Simple, right?

Through the thought experiment of the 25-to-25 problem, my students have now discovered one of the most fundamental—and yet little-known—concepts in personal finance, that of *smoothing consumption*. This principle holds that to maintain the highest possible standard of living over the course of your life, you should calculate the value of your lifetime resources and smooth your consumption over your lifetime. That is, *borrow* when necessary, typically early in life, and *save* when necessary, typically later in life, so that you create (in the language of economics) a *uniform and smooth consumption stream*. I call this concept Long Division because, like the long division you learned as children, it also helps us divide large numbers (our total human capital) into equal portions. In this case, you are dividing the large number of your total lifetime income into the smaller equal portions that represent your yearly spending.

The idea of practicing Long Division, or smoothing consumption based on your *total* capital, over your lifetime, can be traced back to Nobel Laureate and economics professor Franco Modigliani. He, together with a number of co-authors in the 1950s and 1960s, was the first to carefully formulate and test empirically whether people were actually behaving this way. Now, whether most people rationally sum their entire lifetime wages and use that figure as a guide for financial decision-making is one of the most controversial and hotly debated topics in economics departments at major universities around the world. The behavioral school of thought, led by scholars such as Professor Richard Thaler at the University of Chicago, believes that only Mr. Spock (from TV's *Star Trek*) can consistently make decisions in this way. For this school of thought, it is clear that few people can practice what I have described as Long Division, even when all that's required is basic addition and subtraction. Other, more classical economists, argue to salvage the rational life cycle view by explaining away anomalous individual behavior as quirks and blips, small—not conclusive—flaws in the overall rational context of human decision making.

I, personally, don't want to get into the debate of whether the majority of people, or the ones that set prices and actually matter, are rational. This is beyond my pay grade and outside the domain of this book! What I would like to say is that valuing human capital, Long Division, and smoothing provide an excellent *guide* for making the most important financial decisions in your life.

There is evidence that many people actually do follow this idealistic principle, but many others do not. In this chapter, we'll look at how this concept is brought to life by different people.

How Does Income Smoothing (Long Division) Work in Practice?

To understand how this concept might work in practice and how it affects saving and investing behavior, let's imagine the following situation: You are 25, and from the age of 25 to 34 (the next ten years), you know with perfect certainty that you will earn no more (and no less) than $25,000 per year. Then, between ages 35 and 54, your peak earning years, your income will quadruple to $100,000 per year. Finally, at age 55 you will leave the paid workforce, and from ages 55 to 84, you will receive (a pension of) $25,000 per year. (Let's ignore taxes and inflation and interest on money for the moment.)

Hang in there because it's going to get a bit technical. Table 2.1 shows your income flows over your lifetime (in the life you imagine, that is).

TABLE 2.1   Hypothetical Income Smoothing and Savings Rates over a 60-Year Lifecycle: Is this Prudent?

Age	Salary	Spending	Implied Saving Rate
25 to 34 (10 years)	$25,000	$50,000	−100%
35 to 54 (20 years)	$100,000	$50,000	50%
55 to 84 (30 years)	$25,000	$50,000	−100%

If this were you, how, exactly, would you plan your financial life? Would you live cheaply for the first ten years, spend freely for the following twenty, and then go back to consuming only $25,000 per year? You can see the similarities between this situation and our hypothetical inheritance, earlier in the chapter. You can also see that the "pauper/prosper/pauper" lifestyle doesn't make much sense. Instead, the fundamental principle of Long Division, or income smoothing, suggests that you live beyond your immediate (income) means early in life and later in life, and then make it up with large savings during the middle years.

Here's how this would work in practice.

Taking a look at our table, if you add up the 10 years of income at $25,000, plus the 20 years of income at $100,000, plus the $25,000 in the final 30 years, you get a total income (undiscounted) of exactly $3,000,000. Then, if you divide this number by the 60 years ahead of you (from ages 25 to 85), you get an average income of $50,000 per year. What if you spent $50,000 every year for the next 60 years, under the assumption you are earning that amount, on average, over the course of your life? Well, if you assume your investments and borrowings are both allowed to accrue at an interest rate of exactly zero, your plan is sustainable.

The assumption of zero interest for both discounting and accumulating is obviously quite unrealistic, but not outrageous. That said, it really does help understand the process of consumption smoothing. Using the language of finance, if you discount the $3,000,000 in lifetime income, it will be equal to the discounted value of $3,000,000 in lifetime spending. In general, though, under positive interest rates, this will not be the case.

Advice That Goes Against the Grain—but Smoothes?

In the example outlined in our table, although your consumption (what you spend) is a constant amount, your savings rate varies considerably over your lifetime. In the first ten years of your career, your saving rate is –100 percent (because you are spending $50K and only making $25K) whereas in the middle years you are saving 50 percent of what you earn. Normally, this savings pattern—negative savings in early life, coupled with high savings in middle age—would be considered poor financial planning advice, which often focuses on saving a fixed percentage of your earnings over time, but it actually makes perfect sense in the context of income smoothing, or Long Division.

If you follow conventional financial planning advice about replacing income in retirement, the individual in my example would be instructed to attempt to replace $70,000 or $80,000 of annual income at retirement. But, really, this provides a surplus of income at retirement, at the expense of a much lower standard of living in the years before retirement. The goal of retirement planning should not be about maintaining a standard of living or arbitrary income amount taken at a given point in time. Rather, your frame of reference should

Detour: A Quick Guide to Discounting

Let's take a closer look at the concept of discounting I've just introduced. (Skip ahead if this concept is already familiar to you.) This idea is actually so simple that you will likely understand it intuitively even if you don't know the math behind it. Consider this example: Say you are offered the option of receiving $10,000 today, or $10,000 in three years. If you are like most people, the choice is easy; you would prefer to receive $10,000 today over receiving it in the future. Why? Because $10,000 today has more value than the same sum received in the future.

But why is this? On one hand, it might appear that the value of $10,000 received today is the same as $10,000 received in the future. After all, the bills have the same face value and add up to the same amount. However, money received now is more valuable because when you receive money today, you have the opportunity to earn interest on it over time. So if you receive $10,000 now, you can invest those funds and earn interest on them, increasing their future value. However, if you receive the $10,000 at some future date, you have no opportunity to invest the funds and earn interest. Instead, the $10,000 is the total future value of the funds. So the present value, or the value today, of those funds is less than $10,000. This process is called discounting. The amount by which a sum received in the future is discounted to get the value today depends on two factors: how long you have to wait to receive the funds, and the interest rate it is assumed you can earn on the funds if you receive them today.

In the example I gave in which you have total lifetime income of $3,000,000, any economic analysis would require that you "discount" the value of the income you will earn in future years. The process of discounting is the same as the one I've just outlined. If you need $50,000 in income in a future year, the value of those funds today is less than $50,000. Accordingly, if you are earning $25,000 but spending $50,000, but that $50,000 is borrowed from future earnings, you actually need to borrow less than $50,000.

be much wider to include your *lifetime* earning—the fruits of your human capital over your life course—compared to your *lifetime* liabilities and spending.

My point here is that despite all the odd and simplifying assumptions I have made in my example—no death, no taxes, no inflation, no uncertainty, and zero interest rates—it is clear that telling people to save, *just for the sake of saving*, makes no sense. Instead, the more rational approach is to save so that you can smooth consumption over your lifetime, especially when earnings are low. You should be comparing the lifetime income resources available to you (that is, your human capital) to your lifetime liabilities and adjust your spending so the two are relatively close to each other. In fact, economist Lawrence Kotlikoff, chair of the Department of Economics at Boston University, has developed a software program that is designed to assist people in planning to smooth their consumption over time to implement a sustainable life plan. The software, ESPlanner (for "Economic Security Planner")[1] provides a way to model changing financial circumstances along with detailed Social Security and income tax analysis to make recommendations on the amount of retirement savings and life insurance needed to maintain a given standard of living throughout your lifetime. I've also provided a calculator at www.qwema.ca to help you work through a life-cycle smoothing exercise.

We Are Not Mr. Spock in Star Trek

Now, some of you might be thinking: All of this Long Division business might work in the world of classical economists, in which humans are always rational—or in the world of Spock, from TV's *Star Trek*. ("Seems logical to me, Captain.") What can change in practice?

Well, you might not know with certainty that you will earn $100,000 per year in your peak 20 years. It might be more and it might be less. So, you would probably want to compensate for this risk by spending a bit less than $50,000 early on, and then ramping

---

1. The software was co-developed with Jagadeesh Gokhale, a senior fellow at the Cato Institute. See www.esplanner.com for more information.

up, slowly, if things turn out well. Likewise, what if, like most people, you can't borrow at the zero percent interest rate I mentioned earlier? What if you can't get low-cost credit and must repay what you've borrowed using high-cost credit cards charging 25 percent per year, or worse? Then, yes, you would want to avoid dis-saving (or "negative saving") early in life. You might be concerned about health care, or extreme longevity, or mortgage debt, and these are all topics I discuss later.

Alternatively, you might be in an environment of abnormally low interest rates in which you can borrow at negative real (inflation adjusted) rates; in which case your discounted human capital value might be actually higher, and your Long Division process leads to a greater standard of living today.

Back to our example. To be clear, developing good financial habits, such as saving a portion of income, while you are young will probably help you during your entire life. But let's be careful to distinguish between financial advice and psychological or behavioral advice. For now, my key message is that advising the young to save, save, save, just for the sake of it; or advising the middle age to target a given income replacement rate at retirement, as if that point in time matters, is inconsistent with human capital thinking. (Kotlikoff calls these standard recommendations "rules of dumb" because they don't provide a reliable basis for financial planning.) Instead, the concept of Long Division is the rational response to the conventional messages.

In the next section you see that many people have trouble behaving rationally when it comes time to allocating their lifetime resources.

Do People Who Win the Lottery Behave Rationally?

Now that you've seen the rationale for income smoothing, you may be wondering: Do people actually do this in practice? Are people rational with their financial expenditures? Sadly, the answer is often no. For many people, suddenly gaining access to a large lump sum of money—by winning the lottery, for example—can actually make them worse off in the end. This is not just anecdotal evidence or some sensational story of squandered wealth: An interesting study conducted

Detour: Interest Rates and Discounting

But why would the discounted value of your human capital be higher when interest rates are low? I'll take a minute to explain this here. (Feel free to skip ahead if you are already familiar with the concept of discounting. Sometimes it can be tedious to explain this.) Recall that the present value of a sum of money to be received at a future date is determined by discounting the future value using the interest rate the money could earn over the period between today and when it is actually received.

Let's use the example of a T-bill you purchase at issue and hold to maturity. The price you pay for your T-bill is discounted at the time of purchase. That is, you pay something less than the "face" (or par) value of the bill.

When you hold the T-bill to maturity, and are repaid the face value, the difference between what you paid and the amount you are repaid represents the interest on the T-bill. When interest rates are high, the amount of interest you will earn on your T-bill is also high; thus there is a bigger discount at the time of purchase. When interest rates are low, the discount on your T-bill is small because your bill is not going to earn much interest during the holding period.

In an environment of low interest rates, you might purchase a 13-week T-bill with a face value of $10,000 for $9,800. Then, at the end of the 13 weeks, you receive a payment of $10,000, the full face value. The $200 difference between what you paid and what you received at maturity represents the interest you earned during the holding period. In this example, the interest rate was a little more than 2 percent ($200 / $9,800 = 2.04 percent) for 13 weeks, or about 8 percent for a year.

In contrast, when interest rates are high, the discount on your T-bill would be greater. Let's say you purchased the same 13-week T-bill, with a face value of $10,000, for $9,350. At maturity, when you receive your $10,000, fully $650 of that sum represents the interest on your investment. In this example, the interest rate is just under 7 percent ($650 / $9,350 = 6.95 percent) for 13 weeks, or about 28 percent for a year.

In the same way, the value of your human capital is higher in a low interest rate environment. Because interest rates are not significantly discounting the value of your future earnings as they reach maturity (so to speak) and are cashed out by you from year to year, each year of your future earnings is worth more today. This way of thinking might seem a little unusual at first, but it makes sense!

among lottery winners in the State of Florida backs this up with some sobering evidence. First, some background.

During the period from 1993 to 2002, approximately 35,000 people were first-time winners in Florida's popular Fantasy5 lottery game. And, although the median sum won was somewhere between $10,000 and $50,000; about 250 people won between $100,000 and $150,000—and 153 were lucky enough to get more than $150,000. So, these are not trivial sums. You would expect them to have a joyous impact on the winners and a positive effect on their personal finances. (By the way, these numbers are quite accurate because the U.S. Internal Revenue Service requires that all winnings above $600 be reported to them directly by the lottery organizers. Indeed, the information about the names, addresses, county of residence, and winnings is publicly available.)

Did the winners' financial lives improve or worsen after their wins? Some clever researchers at Vanderbilt University set out to explore, using data on Florida lottery winners, whether the financial lives of these lucky few improved after their jackpots.[2] Granted, coming to a consensus on how an "improved financial situation" is defined can be difficult. However, one measure of financial well-being that is both easy to define and easy to collect information about is bankruptcy. The authors of the Vanderbilt study obtained the electronic records for all personal bankruptcies filed in Florida over a period of more than 20 years: from early 1985 (well before the first person studied won the lottery) all the way to late 2007, when the last individual in the lottery database received his or her winnings.

---

2.   Hankins, Hoekstra, and Skiba, "The Ticket to Easy Street?"

At first glance, these two databases—people winning the lottery and people filing for bankruptcy protection—might seem unrelated to each other. Although one might expect that a mere $600 wouldn't help those in financial distress escape or avoid bankruptcy filing, what about those who received $50,000 or $100,000 in found money? You wouldn't normally expect lottery winners to declare bankruptcy after their jackpots, would you? In fact, you might expect the reverse—that they'd be among the least likely to file for bankruptcy protection.

By now, I suspect you know where I'm going.

To carefully measure the financial impact of "sudden and large sums of money" on the financial health of the winners, the researchers split the lottery winners into three groups. *Small winners* were defined as those who won less than $10,000. *Moderate winners* received between $10,000 and $50,000, and *large winners* won jackpots from $50,000 to $150,000.

First, here is a sobering fact about the bankruptcy filing rate. Although the bankruptcy rate in Florida held steady overall at about 0.5 percent for the adult population, the rate for lottery winners was *almost double* the rate for the adult population. This is an average across all winners and across time. But as it turns out, this is not the most alarming finding from the research!

The Perils of Not Smoothing

What the study also found was that among the medium and large lottery winners, the bankruptcy rate dropped significantly in the first two years after winning (by 27 percent and 50 percent, respectively). Indeed, the extra and unexpected money presumably enabled them to pay down debts, repair their budgets, and bring their financial houses into order. Unfortunately, just three to five years after winning, *the situation for large winners was actually worse* than if they had not won the lottery. Not only was the large winner just as likely to file for bankruptcy, but also the rate of bankruptcy filing among this group was quadruple that of the general population. In aggregate, it seems that receiving large financial windfalls only *delays* bankruptcy rather than prevents it.

Let me rephrase this just to be clear: Winning a large and unexpected sum of money was actually hazardous to the financial health of the winners! The first two years—with an extra 50 or 150 grand—was, in a word, grand. But in the next year or so, for a relatively large group of these lottery winners, things got worse than they were before they won the lottery. This is not just a statement about probabilities and frequencies. The bankruptcy database enabled the researchers to compare the level of assets and liabilities of various filers for bankruptcy at the time of filing. What they found was that the net assets of those who received $25,000 to $150,000 were only $8,000 higher than those who won small amounts of less than $1,500. More specifically, small winners in the group who filed for bankruptcy reported unsecured debt of approximately $59,000 when they filed, compared to unsecured debt of $52,000 for large winners. *Where in the world did all the large winners' money go?*

Now, you might question whether anything can be learned from a study limited to bankrupt lottery winners. Others might question whether anything can be learned from a group of less than 2,000 individuals, which is the overlap between the lottery and bankruptcy datasets. You could even argue that people who are in financial distress or on the verge of filing for bankruptcy might increase the frequency and amount they spend on gaming, in hopes of a bailout win. Indeed, the bankruptcy laws in the State of Florida provide for a homestead exemption that allows most bankruptcy filers to keep their houses. Perhaps the lottery winners planned to "game the system" by purchasing principal residences, which can't be seized in the event of bankruptcy, or paying off mortgages—and only then spending to the point of bankruptcy.

However, the researchers were careful to control for this possibility (using a variety of statistical tricks that I will not delve into here).[3] The results indicate that there was no effort to shelter winnings strategically. Instead, it seems apparent that at the end of the day a large and statistically significant number of lottery-winning individuals grossly mismanaged their random good fortune. Instead of saving an extra dollar of found money, they spent it and another one or two

---

3. If you are inclined, I urge you to read the paper "The Ticket to Easy Street?"

dollars along the way. *These individuals did not practice Long Division by smoothing their consumption*, and their irrational approach actually left them worse off than before.

The Smoothest Population of All

Similar results have been documented with other groups (not limited to lottery winners) and other circumstances (with, for example, U.S. federal government rebate checks.) The evidence from these studies is clear: People generally use unexpected windfalls to reduce some debt, initially. But, eventually, they go back to the exact same level of indebtedness. Many just don't plan or think ahead. This is one of the reasons that courts in both the United States and Canada, when awarding damages in the case of negligence and injury judgments, have moved away from large lump-sum judgments to structured settlements that are paid out over time. In the language of the authors of the lottery study: "Policymakers ought to use considerable caution in giving additional resources to heavily indebted individuals with the hope of increasing their financial well-being." I will return to this theme and a discussion of the value of annuities over cash payouts later in the book (in our look at pensions and retirement planning).

Although thousands of lottery winners in Florida don't appear to behave rationally when it comes to their financial affairs, this result is by no means universal nor is it a fact of life for low income-earners. A recent study of the ultra-poor population in West Africa, India, and Bangladesh, published by a group of economists in their recent book *Portfolios of the Poor*,[4] seems to indicate behavior in distant cultures and places that is the exact opposite of our lottery winners.

The authors' in-depth study of 250 families focused on the financial planning abilities of a rather overlooked segment of the world's population, those earning less than $2 USD per day on average. This group, it turns out, suffers from highly irregular and unpredictable income flows that are dependent on events outside their immediate control. During some days and even weeks, these families earned no

---

4. Collins, Morduch, Rutherford, and Ruthven, *Portfolios of the Poor: How the World's Poor Live on $2 a Day.*

income at all, and at other times, they earned more than their average of $2 in a given day. (In other words, their average earnings were $2 per day, but with huge swings, or in the language of statisticians, a very large standard deviation.)

And yet, despite these erratic circumstances, the authors found that few of these families consumed based on their immediate, daily earnings only. Instead, on days for which income was greater than average, they set aside (relatively) substantial sums of money and did not spend it. This fund served as a reserve for days in which they didn't earn anything. By drawing on their reserve, on days when they earned less than average, they would still consume relatively the same amount compared to the days when things were better.

Now, although this seems like a commonsense solution preached by any parent who has admonished his offspring to save for a rainy day, the level of consistency in implementing this practice among the world's poorest families, in such dire circumstances, seems remarkable. Overall, the authors claim that the consumption profile of the world's poorest families over their life cycle was relatively smooth *and* based on an average of their meager daily earnings. In other words: they practice Long Division.

Indeed, according to a review of the book in *The Economist*, "The subjects used a combination of loans and savings to ensure their lives were not, literally, hostage to fortune. Hardly anyone lived utterly hand to mouth." The review went on to say, "The research provides evidence of the sophistication with which poor people think about their finances."[5] It would seem that their behavior could serve as a financial inspiration to us all.

Where Does All of This Leave Us?

One can speculate only whether our bankrupt lottery winners—and possibly all lottery winners—would be better off financially, in the very long run, if their winnings were specified or perhaps even mandated in an annuity (periodic income) form, as opposed to a single lump sum. And, although I'm sure some would convert their

---

5. "Smooth Operators," *The Economist*.

annuities into (much smaller) lump sums, hence unraveling any policy benefits, it certainly makes me wonder whether money can actually be hazardous to your wealth.

At the very least, perhaps it's a blessing in disguise that our most valuable asset, human capital, can be monetized only slowly and with great effort. Indeed, if you could take infinite advances against our future labor income and sell it all in the marketplace today, you would much likely be worse off in the long term. In the meantime, perhaps the most rational approach to maximizing your financial well-being over your lifetime is *not* to plan for a lottery win but to adopt the perspectives of the world's poorest people in planning your spending over time.

In this chapter you have learned what is probably the most fundamental axiom within *strategic* personal financial planning for individuals, and that is the notion of consumption smoothing. That is, every financial (and insurance) decision that you make in your life should be motivated by the objective of removing the jagged corners and rough edges in life. More on this in later chapters.

Summary: The Four Principles in Action

- Long DIVISION provides a fresh, strongly intuitive, and useful perspective that can potentially better outcomes at each stage of life: early on, when you are investing in human capital during your income-earning years, and long into retirement.

- Long Division encourages us to use the simple tools of ADDITION and SUBTRACTION to take a holistic view of our lifetime earnings and liabilities, smoothly steering our day-to-day spending.

- Much of conventional financial planning rules-of-thumb are not quite rational; for example, the idea of replacing 70 percent of your salary at retirement. This rule relies on inappropriate MULTIPLICATION of income later in life to set retirement saving goals. Instead, you should put your focus on DIVIDING your resources over time.

- The evidence also shows that simply ADDING income (in the form of sudden financial windfalls) does not necessarily improve our standards of living over time—lottery winners in Florida do a worse job of managing cash than do the world's poorest citizens.

3

How Much Debt Is Too Much and How Much Is Too Little?

As you learned in the previous chapter, it makes little economic sense to target a fixed or unyielding savings rate (while you are working) or replacement rate (for income in retirement). Instead, the correct way of thinking about saving rates is as the output of a financial plan that seeks to *smooth consumption* or equally distribute the benefits of human capital over the entire life cycle. That is: When you are young, have few financial resources, and are investing time to develop and improve your human capital, spending more than you earn is, in fact, quite rational. Similarly, during your middle and later working years, when your earnings are likely the highest they will ever be, it makes sense to save at much higher rates than normally advocated. All of this I introduced in the last chapter, and I called this process Long Division. Now, critical to the successful application of the Long Division process is the ability to borrow money at reasonable rates, whether it is to buy a house, finance a car, or invest in education.

In this chapter, I take a much closer look at the borrowing process. I won't particularly focus on the *amount* of debt Americans have on their personal balance sheets, but rather the puzzling phenomena of how Americans *diversify* their debts and thereby fail to optimize their overall debt management strategies. Right now, the ways people use debt inhibit success with Long Division. Let's delve into what's going on and how (and why) you can do better.

Americans Have Diverse Debts

Recall that according to data from the Survey of Consumer Finances (SCF) conducted in 2007, close to 77 percent of American households had some type of debt on their financial balance sheet. In 2007, those who had debts owed a median $69,000 to their creditors.[1] This number is estimated to have risen approximately 180 percent over the last 18 years and is now 50 percent higher than it was at the beginning of the decade.[2] The trend line has been moving upward regardless of whether debt is examined relative to income or assets. Since 1989, the real growth of household debt has outpaced the growth of income by an annualized rate of 5 percent, and it has outpaced the growth of assets by 3 percent.

Americans also have a wide *variety* of debt. For example, debts and liabilities can be held as mortgages, lines of credit, student loans, and vehicle loans—and credit cards and other installment debts. Table 3.1 provides a summary of the various debts held by American families.

Note that 46 percent of Americans have a mortgage on a principal residence, and 46 percent have credit card debt. The average size of the principal residence mortgage, for those who actually had a mortgage, was $152,988. These numbers do not include the informal debt markets in which money is owed to friends, relatives, community charities, and so on.

Only recently, as a result of the financial crisis, has the overall savings rate increased. Right now it stands at just under 6 percent (in

---

1. Figures in 2009 dollars.
2. According to the most recent Survey of Financial Security (2005), the median amount of debt held by Canadian households increased by 37.5 percent since 1999 and equaled to $47,500 (2009 dollars). The median amounts of debt and the percentages of Canadians that have them are as follows: mortgages ($99.4K, 36.5 percent), lines of credit ($9.6K, 24.9 percent), credit cards ($2.6K, 39.3 percent), student loans ($9.6K, 11.8 percent), vehicle loans ($11.8K, 25.8 percent), and other types of debt ($6.4K, 14.1 percent). See Statistics Canada, *The Wealth of Canadians*.

TABLE 3.1   What do American Families Owe, and to Whom do They Owe It?

	Median	Average	% With This Type of Debt
	$	$	%
Main Residence Mortgage	111,618	152,988	46.3
Other Real Estate Mortgage	102,401	182,070	5.5
Line of credit (Unsecured)	3,891	24,679	1.7
Credit card	3,072	7,475	46.1
Student loans	12,288	22,016	15.2
Vehicle loans	11,776	14,951	34.9
Other debt	5,120	15,667	6.8
Sum of Percentages:			**156.5**
Total Debt in any Form:	**68,916**	**129,026**	**77**

early 2009), which is much higher than the rate of -0.4 percent reported by the U.S. Department of Commerce for 2005.[3]

These Eggs Belong in One Basket

Now, this might not be what jumps out at you from scanning that table, but what I see—and what concerns me about current levels of debt—is the extent to which Americans are *diversifying their debt* by having multiple liabilities at differing interest rates, instead of using their income and savings to minimize their borrowing costs.

To understand the phenomenon of "debt diversification," look again at our table. Notice that the numbers in the last column add up to 156.5 percent, or more than 100 percent. What this tells us is that some people owe money to at least two different creditors, and perhaps even

3. Source: U.S. Commerce Department News Releases, August 2008 and April 2009. In Canada, the personal savings rate was 1.2 percent in 2005 and 4.7 percent in the first quarter of 2009. Canadian data from Statistics Canada, "Economic indicators, by province and territory (monthly and quarterly)," from CANSIM tables 079-0003 and 080-0014.

more. In fact, the greater the sum of percentages is here, the larger the fraction of the population that has more than one type of liability.

Many students, for example, borrow from banks using a personal line of credit, have credit cards, and participate in government student loan programs. Now, many of these students might not have much choice and are essentially forced to borrow from various sources. Nevertheless, the evidence suggests that a large segment of the borrowing population *is* able to consolidate and optimize their debt, yet chooses not to.

I suspect that people might be spreading their debts across various creditors—even in the absence of any liquidity constraints (which are limits on the amount you can borrow)—to fulfill an unconscious desire to compartmentalize their liabilities (that is, to break the total amount down into easier-to-swallow chunks). Or perhaps this is a remnant from our approach to asset management, in which we are told *not* to place all our investment eggs in one basket.

Today, with interest rates at historically low levels and many Americans fretting about the prospect of higher rates going forward, I believe it is important to deflect consumers' attention away from speculating on the direction of interest rates and more toward examining their own personal financial balance sheets. Optimal debt management strategies can and should be implemented independently of the direction of short-term rates.

Optimal Debt Management Strategies Across Space and Time

The anecdotal evidence I have encountered is consistent with what the sparse data suggests. Informal discussions with financial planners and retail bankers indicate that many of you choose to rely on various sources of debt, often on an ongoing basis, as opposed to keeping all your debts aggregated in one account. For example: your neighbor might be running a credit card balance and making monthly home mortgage payments, while financing a vehicle and drawing down a line of credit for renovations, all at different interest rates.

This practice—many different debts at many different rates—illustrates one dimension of a flawed debt management strategy: *debt diversification across space silos.* Another dimension of poor debt management can be labeled *debt diversification across time.* This refers to the tendency of consumers to hold and deposit income dollars in a low-interest (taxable) bank accounts rather than using the funds to reduce outstanding debt balances immediately, in which the interest charge accumulates at higher ("non-tax-deductible") rates. Clearly, it is not rational to diversify debts across either space silos or time (giving rise to what economists call *a cash-flow mismatch*), especially when cheaper debt management strategies are readily available. The benefits of making an aggregate debt repayment to a single creditor can be substantial. This might be obvious to many, yet it is not widely practiced, perhaps because the magnitude of the cost of not implementing this strategy is not well understood.

Liability Silos Compared

According to the 2007 Survey of Consumer Finances, the average U.S. household carries a credit card balance of $7,500 (2009 dollars). I will use this number in the numerical example to follow. Let's further assume (just for the sake of this example) that a consumer has an additional $7,500 balance outstanding on a line of credit. If this family can only afford to make a constant payment of $200 per month in each of these accounts, *how long will it take to pay down each type of debt* and *how much will it cost?*

Research shows that the average credit card charges an annual percentage rate of 15 percent. A typical secured line of credit would charge 3.25 percent, based on the current (June 2009) prime rate of interest. However, some people cannot borrow at average rates. Accordingly, here are prepared scenarios with average rates (for credit cards) and prime rates (for lines of credit), and suboptimal (higher) rates for both debt instruments. All the rates, however, are assumed to remain constant over time.

Table 3.2 illustrates how long it would take to eliminate the balance on each account (or debt silo) assuming the same initial balances of $7,500 and identical payments of $200 per month.

TABLE 3.2   How Many Months Does it Take to Pay Off a Debt of $7,500 in $200 Monthly Increments and What is the Total Cost?

Account	Months	Sum of Cash Flows
Line of credit (3.25%)	40	$ 7,891
Line of credit (5.25%)	41	$ 8,153
Credit card (15%)	51	$ 10,009
Credit card (18%)	55	$ 10,852

The results are as follows: It takes 40 months to pay off the line of credit under a 3.25 percent rate and 41 months under the 5.25 percent rate. In contrast, it takes 51 months to eliminate the credit card debt charging 15 percent and a whopping 55 months to pay off the credit card charging 18 percent. The total amount paid will vary for each form of debt and interest rate. It ranges from $7,891 for the lower interest line of credit to $10,852 for the retail credit card—a difference of $2,961. Accordingly, if this customer can choose to hold her debt at 3.25 percent versus 18 percent, she will save nearly $3,000—or 40 percent of the original debt amount—by using the line of credit.

Now, if you go even further and assume a hypothetical consumer who has three different types of debt: two credit cards (with rates of 15 percent and 18 percent) and a line of credit (charging 3.25 percent)—all with the exact same hypothetical balance, the benefits would be even more pronounced. In total, all the payments that must be made to pay off the three accounts, that is, the line of credit and the two credit cards at their respective rates, is $28,752. However, if all three accounts were consolidated into the line of credit (that is, *not* diversified), the payments would only total 3 x $7,891 = $23,672, which represents potential savings of $5,080 over the life of the liabilities. In addition, the total amount of debt would be eliminated faster, saving 16 months, compared to waiting 55 months until the last payment on the retail credit card is made. Alternatively, transferring the credit card balances to the (higher) 5.25 percent line of credit, versus holding three separate accounts would result in total payments of $24,460; leading to total savings of $4,292.

You might be interested to look at the effects of debt diversification in your own life. I've created a calculator at www.qwema.ca that enables you to enter and compare various debt scenarios, calculating the impact of any debt diversification you are doing now and the effects any debt consolidation can make for you.

It is important to stress that the point of this analysis is *not* to zero-in on credit card companies and high interest rates, but rather to illustrate the benefits of optimal debt management. The numerical results would be comparable if you used a car loan, student loan, or even a personal loan charging similar interest rates.

Another interesting study that sheds light on the avoidable and unnecessary financing costs incurred by many consumers comes from an article recently published in the *American Economic Review*.[4] For this article, the authors tracked every credit card and checking transaction completed by a group of almost 1,000 households over a two-year period. The authors' intent was to identify all the costs these households could (theoretically) have avoided by simply making different, more intelligent decisions using the credit cards and accounts they already had. Examples of foregone savings opportunities uncovered in their research included people who allowed interest to accrue on a credit card, while extra cash sat idle in a bank account that could have paid down a portion of the debt. Others included individuals with different credit cards, each with different interest rates, and all carrying a balance, even though the lowest-rate card had available credit. (Earlier in the chapter, I called this debt diversification.) Yet other examples included people paying checking account fees for an account with a zero balance, and overdraft fees on their bank account when they could have used a much cheaper source of credit such as a credit card.

The interesting finding from this research study was that these careless practices were not rare, nor were they of trivial magnitude. The hypothetical annual savings per household amounted to hundreds of dollars on average, and in some cases, it was in the thousands of dollars. Once again, the evidence suggests that there are intelligent ways to manage debt, and there are careless ways. Within the context of Long

---

4. Stango and Zinman, "What Do Consumers Really Pay on Their Checking and Credit Card Accounts?"

Division, debt *per se* is not imprudent or irresponsible. There is nothing wrong with smoothing consumption by borrowing money (especially when you are young) *provided you are smart about how you manage your financial affairs*. And evidence from this study shows that the savings can be measured in thousands of dollars.

Bottom Line: Debt Diversification Destroys Value

I am careful to shy away from preaching the virtues of debt-free living or lamenting the increasing debt load over the last decade. My analyses and the framework of Long Division takes for granted the necessity, inevitability, and benefit of debt. My agenda is more straightforward: first, to point out the extent of debt diversification and second, to quantify the benefits of consolidating debt. This chapter identifies two distinct dimensions of inappropriate debt-management strategies. The first dimension is debt diversification across space (different silos). The second dimension comes from mismanaging debt levels across time, in which salary income and deposits sit in low (or zero) interest accounts while the debt clock is ticking at much higher rates. Both forms of debt diversification destroy value.

I think that the prevalence of debt diversification can be traced to what behavioral economists label the existence of *mental accounts*. According to the work of Nobel Prize-winning economist Daniel Kahneman and his co-researcher Richard H. Thaler, investors tend to segregate and manage their investment holdings in distinct "lock-boxes" or silos.[5] They make decisions within each of these investment lock-boxes without taking into account the interaction between them. Thus, for example, investors avoid realizing investment losses on a particular brokerage account because they want to "close it out" at a profit. Or consumers create and adhere to budgets for various financial expenditures but structure the boundaries between these individual activities arbitrarily. Or people set a financial goal to pay off their mortgage within 10 or 15 years, even if it means incurring other debts and liabilities at higher rates along the way.

---

5. See Thaler and Sunstein, *Nudge*.

The same behavioral phenomena are evident with personal debts and liabilities. Consumers might be keeping their diversified debts in small mental accounts—perhaps to avoid the "sticker shock" of getting one statement with a very large balance—even though these debts can easily be consolidated. If the interest rates underlying the different silos were identical and the payment terms were the same, this practice would be harmless. However, in a world of differing interest rates, small payments over prolonged periods can add up to substantial sums.

Should You Borrow from Yourself?

The problem of inefficient debt management via diversification doesn't just manifest itself in the odd mix of liabilities on the right side of an individual's personal balance sheet. In fact, the same problem occurs when individuals have credit card and other consumer loans at high rates, when they could easily tap into (and sell some of) their investments to pay off these loans instead. One example is 401(k) loans.[6] At first glance, advising people to borrow from their 401(k) plan seems inappropriate and inadvisable except for extreme circumstances. No self-respecting financial commentator would advocate this as a first resort. And yet, research suggests that Americans collectively could save billions of dollars yearly if they did exactly that. Let me explain.

Two economists at the Federal Reserve Board carefully examined data from the U.S. Survey of Consumer Finance (SCF), a dataset you previously saw. In particular, they looked at households who had various outstanding debts, such as credit cards, lines of credit, and consumer loans but who also had a 401(k) plan that allowed them to borrow. Borrowing from the 401(k) obligates you to repay the sum of funds withdrawn over approximately two or three years, but without any additional interest cost or tax penalties. In other words, you have to pay back only principal. Thus, in theory, borrowing from your 401(k) deprives the missing investments (the withdrawn funds) from growing

---

6. These are similar to group RRSPs in Canada. However, you can't borrow against the assets or from group RRSPs. You can withdraw the funds from an individual RRSP to pay off high-interest debt, but this is a taxable event that complicates the analysis and relative benefit.

at the same rate as the rest of the investments in the plan. However, if the rate of interest you are paying on your debt exceeds a reasonable estimate of this return, it actually makes sense to borrow from the 401(k) instead of from other sources. Why? Because your personal balance sheet will improve by swapping debts within the various silos.

When these economists began their study, they did not expect to find many people who could actually borrow from their 401(k) plans but chose instead to carry high-interest debt. And yet, this is exactly what they did find. People preferred to carry high-interest debt rather than borrow from their 401(k), even though it would save them money in the long run.

Here are some summary statistics. In 2004, the most recent data available to the authors, approximately 46 percent of surveyed households reported having a 401(k) plan. The ability to borrow from a 401(k) is something that is determined by the plan sponsors and the company, and approximately 32 percent of households reported the ability to take loans from their 401(k) plan. However, a mere 5 percent of surveyed households reported having an outstanding 401(k) plan loan. This is a small fraction of the total household population, but it has actually doubled over the previous 12 years. Stated differently, the loan rate among eligible households was 16 percent. The median outstanding loan balance was $4,000.[7]

The main insight from their study, which should resonate with the results of the previous section, is that a much higher percentage of eligible households had outstanding consumer debts, likely at relatively higher interest rates given the cost of maintaining credit cards and other such loans.

The authors claim that approximately 40 percent to 60 percent of eligible households, depending on the assumptions used, would gain from restructuring household debt and borrowing from 401(k) plans instead. Ultimately, the authors estimate that U.S. households could have shifted more than $9 billion in debt, which is $3,400 per household, to save $3.3 billion collectively, or an average of $200 per household per year.

One rather ironic positive aspect of the recent credit crisis and the greater difficulty many consumers are experiencing in obtaining

---

7. Stango and Zinman

consumer debt is they will likely increase the amount they borrow from their 401(k) plans, simply because they have no other alternative. On the one hand, this act will clearly diminish and reduce the long-term value of their retirement savings. And yet, this likely implies they will not be paying high interest rates. Only time will tell whether the good (lower rates) offsets the bad (lower retirement balances).

The Borrowing Sweet Spot: Age 53

Although it seems many people are making expensive financial mistakes when it comes to borrowing money and the rates they pay, it appears that age has something important to do with it. In fact, researchers at Harvard University and the Federal Reserve Bank of Chicago found that it seems you will be paying the "best rates" on your debt at precisely the age of 53.[8] If you are younger or older, you can expect to pay more. Odd result? Let me explain.

Going far beyond the Survey of Consumer Finances data, the authors merged a massive panel dataset from a number of national and international financial institutions. They looked at a number of financial choices people make about borrowing from a variety of different countries, not just the United States (and including places like Argentina). For example, they examined data on rates paid for home equity loans (these are similar to a mortgage) and home equity lines of credit and car loans and small business credit cards.

They also conducted a rather clever study on credit card balance transfers. In this study, the authors examined (anonymously, hopefully) the records of about 15,000 people who transferred credit card balances from (high-interest) cards to "teaser offer" low-interest cards. Note that the teaser rates apply only to the transferred balance and not new purchases. Moreover, any payments made on the new credit card go toward paying down the transferred balance loan (at low rates) as opposed to the new purchase balance (at standard rates).

---

8. Agarwal, Driscoll, Gabaix, and Laibson, "The Age of Reason: Financial Decisions over the Lifecycle."

It is clear that the smart thing to do while the teaser rate is in force is to continue using the old card for new purchases and avoid using the new card at all, once a balance has been transferred to it. The authors deduced the number of people—and their ages—who behaved smartly after transferring a balance. (All this assumes somebody carrying a balance at all can be described as clever. Presumably they were smoothing consumption.)

The bottom line is that the authors compared financial behavior and the presence of smart financial decisions—such as loan balances, credit scores, general education, and so on. The main research question underlying all their analyses was *At what age do consumers exhibit the best and smartest financial planning behavior?*

The results of their rather exhaustive study across all these different data are remarkably consistent. Thus, for example, they documented that college graduates are "better" at these decisions and hence pay less in total costs compared to high school graduates (yet another reason to invest in human capital). They also found that individuals with graduate degrees made better decisions than those with only a college degree. And yet, there was something about age 53.

In their words: "We find that younger adults and older adults borrow at higher interest rates and pay more fees than middle-aged adults, controlling for all observable characteristics including multiple measures of risk." The researchers documented something they called a "U-shaped pattern" in the price people pay for financial services, and their explanation for this pattern was part behavioral and part biological. They believe the U-shaped pattern comes from a trade-off between wisdom, which comes from experience, and age-related declines in cognitive ability. For the authors, the trade-offs are as follows: younger borrowers lack life experience; however, older adults are sometimes subject to decreasing cognitive capacity.

To sum up, in the words of the authors: "Middle-aged adults may be at a decision making sweet spot. They have substantial amount of practical experience and have not yet had significant cognitive decline."

Oh, and Being Slim Can Help as Well

And, if you are surprised to learn that age 53 is the optimal age in terms of the lowest financing costs, some researchers in Japan have found an even more shocking result: *being skinny pays interest!*[9]

These researchers established a number of rather odd empirical facts, albeit with data that is limited to the Japanese, which perhaps should be interpreted with tongue in cheek. They examined data from the comprehensive Japan Household Survey on Consumer Preferences and Satisfaction in 2005. This provides a comprehensive report of both financial (balance sheet, income statement) and—in contrast to the Survey of Consumer Finances in the U.S.—detailed health metrics for Japanese households. In particular, they focused on body mass index (BMI), which is defined as weight in kilograms divided by height in meters squared. If the BMI value was less than 18.5, the individual was defined as underweight. If the BMI was between 18.5 and 25, the individual was defined as normal. And anything above 25 was considered pre-obese and then, beyond 30, obese. (In Japan, BMI categories are calculated slightly differently than in North America.) This number was then "regressed" (or linked to) whether the individual had any debt. Accordingly, the average BMI for debtors was approximately 23.26, whereas the BMI for non-debtors was 22.7, which was a statistically significant difference.

It seems that debtors are likely to be more obese than nondebtors are; a fact the researchers attributed to what economists label greater "time discounting." In other words, according to the researchers, overweight people tend to be more impatient and would rather consume more today than tomorrow. Hence, although they might like to smooth (a lot) of consumption, they tilt the smoothing toward the present as opposed to the future. A survey administered by the researchers seems to indicate that people with higher BMI values tended to discount at greater personal interest rates and in general exhibited more impatience.

Whether these results are applicable to the United States or Canada is unclear, but one thing is certain: Your human capital will be

---

9. Ikeda, Kang, and Ohtake, "Fat Debtors."

worth much more if you keep consumption both smooth and relatively modest, which can have desirable effects on your waistline, too!

Debt Literacy as Distinct from General Financial Literacy

One last study worth noting, which continues on the "financial mistakes" theme, is an article called "Debt Literacy, Financial Experiences and Overindebtedness" published by the National Bureau of Economic Research in 2009.[10] The authors surveyed levels of financial literacy (from a group of approximately 1,000 U.S. residents) in the general population. They looked in particular at what they called vulnerable demographic groups within the general population, such as the elderly, certain minorities, people with lower incomes and lower net worth, and women. They asked members of these groups various questions to elicit their debt literacy. The exam-style questions were structured to include multiple possible answers and dealt with a variety of issues such as the mathematics of interest rates, credit card mechanics, etc. The results were then graded by the professors who were the authors of the report, as well as the respondents themselves, who were asked to assess their literacy.

Their results are quite sobering and alarming. In their words: "Individuals with lower levels of debt literacy tend to transact in high-cost manners, incurring higher fees.... One third of the charges and fees paid by less-knowledgeable individuals can be attributed to ignorance."

Even more striking was that many of the people who scored poorly on the debt literacy questions actually scored their own knowledge quite highly. In particular, the elderly respondents thought they know much more about interest rates, debts, and credit cards than they demonstrably did!

---

10.   Lusardi and Tutano.

Concluding Thoughts: Is Debt Soothing or Smoothing?

Most financial commentators differentiate between borrowing that is used for investment purposes at relatively low interest rates (aka good debt) and discretionary borrowing used for consumption and expenditures at relatively high interest rates (aka bad debt.) According to the consensus view, *good debt* makes financial sense and should be encouraged in moderation, whereas *bad debt*, resulting from poor financial hygiene (the set of habits, attitudes, and behaviors people have toward managing their finances) should be shunned.

In contrast, I have tried to argue that human capital thinking and holistic balance sheet management results in a different perspective. Yes, I agree that using your credit card to buy yet another gadget you will never use and don't really need is "bad" financial planning. And individuals who are ignorant of the basics of credit card interest rates and compounding periods are paying more than they should and suffer from these financial mistakes.

Yet I believe that much less emphasis should be placed on the purpose of the debt itself or even the absolute rate you pay, and much greater emphasis on getting the best possible rate relative to your individual financial condition and the overall standard of living this creates over the course of your life. Either way, debt isn't evil. It's a tool.

And so, the main question you ask yourself when contemplating going into debt shouldn't be, *Can I afford this particular purchase?* Rather, I suggest you ask yourself, *Will today's purchase, which might be financed by high cost and long-term debt, reduce my **future** standard of living by more than the purchase will increase my **present** standard of living?* If the answer to this second question is yes, or even maybe, the purchase doesn't make sense from a Long Division perspective. On the other hand, if you are relatively secure that your long-term (sometimes called permanent income) is greater than your current income, by all means go ahead and borrow, consume, and enjoy.

Summary: The Four Principles in Action

- Critical to the successful application of Long DIVISION over the life cycle is the ability to borrow money at reasonable rates. Oddly enough, many people behave quite irrationally when it comes to borrowing money. It's not that they borrow too much, but that they tend to pay different rates on different debts and practice an inappropriate diversification strategy.

- There are two aspects of flawed debt MULTIPLICATION strategies: diversification across space silos and diversification across time. Both forms SUBTRACT value from your total net worth.

- The best way to think about debt is not to focus on the ADDITION of debt, but to focus on getting the best possible rate relative to your individual financial condition and the overall smooth standard of living this creates over the course of your life.

4

Are Kids Investments and Can Marriages Diversify?

Of the many questions I ask my undergraduate students during the semester-long course on personal finances, the question I ask to kick-start the lecture on family economics provoke the strongest response. Here they are: Are children financial *assets* or *liabilities*? And, did your parents have you for *consumption* or *investment* purposes?

After the yelling subsides and the classroom returns to normal, I add that I'm sure their parents love them very much (for the most part)—but note that at the same time, my students must acknowledge that kids aren't free, and they can have quite a detrimental impact on a family's personal finances. Here are some facts: According to my much-referenced Survey of Consumer Finances (SCF), in the year 2007 couples without children reported an average net worth of more than $800K, whereas couples with children had an average net worth of only $594K, or about 25 percent less.[1] This gap is not arbitrary or unique to the year 2007: The same pattern can be observed in the 1998, 2001, and 2004 waves of the survey. Moreover, if anything, the gap has been getting larger over time. So, at first glance, it seems that having kids makes you poorer! Now, whether this proves true in the long run, or whether it is a function of the age of the parents surveyed, or whether net worth is measured much too narrowly (after all, the SCF measures only traditional financial capital)—all these

---

1. The median U.S. net worth was $191K for couples without children and $141K for couples with children. In Canada, the numbers are similar: in 2005, the median net worth for couples without children at home was $242,900, which is $53,900 (or 29 percent) more than couples with children under 18, whose net worth was $189,000. For Canadian data, see *The Wealth of Canadians*.

issues are up for debate. However, it seems clear that decisions about marriage and family have financial implications. In this chapter, I devote my attention to the implications of life-cycle thinking, holistic balance-sheet management, and the rule of Long Division to decisions about childbearing and family formation (that is, getting married and having kids, not necessarily in that order).

Children: Explicit Liabilities, Hidden Assets

Like most of the other topics I address in this book, the decision to have (or not to have) children is deeply personal and involves much more than simply dollars and cents. For example, in some cultures, procreation is viewed as a straightforward religious obligation, wholly independent of personal wealth and financial means. The Biblical story of God's commandment to Adam and Eve in Genesis 1:28: *Be fruitful, and multiply, and replenish the earth* can be taken quite literally, as a requirement to have as many children as physically possible. In countries and places around the world, children are an economic necessity because they create another helpful pair of hands within the household, to assist on the family farm or in the fields. Yet other people view a large family as evidence of financial success; a status symbol akin to a large house or expensive car. Still others might not give the question of having children much thought until it is too late. Yet, independent of all other, nonfinancial factors, the financial and economic implications of children cannot and should not be ignored. Why not? Because having children will dramatically alter your holistic balance sheet—perhaps in ways that will surprise you.

According to a survey conducted by the U.S. Department of Agriculture, the average cost of raising a child from birth until 18 is $221,190 for a child born in 2008.[2] (A more precise estimate depends on your individual income and wealth level, mainly due to a variety of

---

2. In Canada, the cost to raise a child from birth to age 18 is estimated at $183K. See Canadian Council on Social Development's *Stats & Facts: Canadian Families* at http://www.ccsd.ca/factsheets/family/index.htm. Figures adjusted for inflation.

tax credits and deductions that are available in the U.S. tax code.) I've included a basic calculator at www.qwema.ca to enable you to estimate the cost today of raising your existing or planned kids to age 18. This range, of course, does not include the escalating cost of college, and it assumes the child actually moves out of the house at the age of 18. (How many kids do that nowadays?)

At first glance, it seems kids are terribly expensive. If this is so, could paying parents to have children increase the supply of kids in a society? Here is but one interesting case.

Inducing More Children

In the mid-1980s, the provincial government in the Canadian province of Quebec became alarmed at the rapid decline in its overall fertility rate (defined as the average number of children born to each female). Historically Quebeckers, with their strong Catholic identity, had large families with sometimes as many as 15 children per household. Without a doubt, they had the largest families and highest fertility rates in Canada.

Demographically, a society needs a fertility rate of 2.1 children per female to maintain a stable population; one that neither grows nor shrinks over time. (The extra 0.1 is needed to account for children that either die prior to giving birth themselves or decide not to have children.) By the mid-1980s, this rate had fallen drastically in Quebec to 1.36 children per female. What this meant, in general terms, is that if there were a total of five million Quebeckers in the current generation, of whom half were male and half female and a birthrate of 1.36 children per woman, one generation from now the population would shrink to 3.4 million Quebeckers. (The 2.5 million males are assumed to have zero offspring—this not as obvious as you might think—and the 2.5 million females would give birth to the 1.36 children each. So, 2.5 million women x 1.36 children per woman = 3.4 million children born.)

Going forward, if you assume half of those 3.4 million new children are male and half female, and those females have 1.36 children each, then the total number of children born in the second generation would be 2.3 million; and so on, as the effects of the low fertility rate worked their way through the population. (I am oversimplifying this discussion, but I trust you get the general picture.) In contemplating the low fertility rate among their shrinking population, the Government of Quebec felt it had to do something, soon, or eventually there would be no more Quebeckers. *The human capital of Quebec was at stake!*

So, and this is where the story becomes relevant to money milestones, in the 1980s the provincial government brought in a program called *The Allowance for Newborn Children* or, as it became known, "bucks for babies." Under this program, parents were paid approximately $500 Canadian (CAD) (slightly less than $500 U.S. dollars) upon the birth of their first child, and $1,000 CAD for their second child. If they had additional children beyond two, they could get much more, as much as $8,000 (nontaxable!) for each birth.

Now, do you think these payouts helped induce fertility and increase the birth rate? Well, you might be surprised that the answer is *not by much*. After all, when you compare a few thousand dollars in government transfers to the potentially hundreds of thousands of dollars in future costs to raise each child, it would be surprising if these sums had any impact at all. In fact, the Government of Quebec opened the cash registers even further with ongoing financial inducements for children and even began to provide universal daycare at greatly subsidized rates. But none of this helped much. Indeed, if the decision not to have children was purely motivated by financial considerations, you would have expected to see greater change to the fertility and birth rate as the cash piled up in the hands of parents.

Interestingly enough, it was only after the provincial government went one step further in 2006 and legislated the most liberal and generous parental leave in the country—that is, the amount of paid time parents can take off work to care for their children—that there started to be some noticeable change in behavior. By 2006, the fertility rate had increased to 1.62 children per female, and the number of births has been rising each year since. The 2008 rate was 1.74, which is the highest rate since 1976. Moreover, although this change might have been a result of all the cumulative inducements, perhaps the ability of working parents to actually stay home and enjoy their children had the greatest impact of all. By the way, as of early 2009, the population of Quebec had risen from 6.6 million in 1985 to nearly 8 million; the supply of human capital is increasing![3] And, raising these kids might not be as costly as you think.

In the next section, you see how children can serve not just as balance sheet liabilities but also as *de facto* pensions for their parents. Sound strange? Read on for some surprising insights.

Children as Pensions—And a General's Revenge

The modern state-funded pension system, like the U.S. Social Security program or the Canada Pension Plan, can be traced back to the German chancellor Otto von Bismarck (1815–1898). Over 125 years ago, back in 1881, he introduced his concept of the first state pension plan to the German parliament. Under his plan, which was adopted in 1889, a basic income would be provided to all retirees when they reached the age of retirement and financed by a tax on workers. (The initial age of retirement proposed by Bismarck and adopted by the German state was 70. The age of retirement was reduced to 65 some 27 years later, in 1916.[4])

Although I discuss pension milestones and retirement income planning in greater detail in the final chapter of this book, at this point I want to explore some general comments about the relationship between pension plans and family dynamics.

Chancellor Bismarck's pension prototype, which was refined by Britain's Sir William Beveridge in the early 1940s, has become known by the acronym PAYGO, for *Pay As You Go*. Under a PAYGO pension, retired workers are supported by, and indirectly receive their

---

3. Statistics on the fertility, population, and birth rates in Quebec are taken from the Institute de la statistique, Quebec; available at www.stat.gouv.gc.ca.

4. There is a persistent myth that Germany adopted age 65 as the standard retirement age because that was Bismarck's age. In fact, Germany initially set age 70 as the retirement age (and Bismarck himself was 74 at the time), and it was not until 27 years later (in 1916) that the age was lowered to 65. By that time, Bismarck had been dead for 18 years. See the brief history at Social Security Online, the official website of the U.S. Social Security Administration: http://www.socialsecurity.gov/history/ottob.html.

pensions from, younger workers still in the labor force. Think of PAYGO pensions as a straight demographic transfer, or like passing the collection plate at church. In a sense, the young (children) support the old (parents), and this compulsory transfer mechanism is enforced and managed by the state.

But for PAYGO pension systems to work efficiently and cheaply, society needs many more (younger) workers in the labor force than retired workers receiving payments. That is, at the most basic level, to pay for workers' pensions, society needs many children. In fact, this is precisely the reason that so many states (including the Canadian province of Quebec, as you previously saw) are preoccupied with increasing fertility rates.

Unfortunately, the pension systems envisioned by Bismarck and Beveridge have not withstood the test of time and are now on shaky ground. In many countries, where fertility rates are quite low, the ratio of retired workers to children is exploding. Thus, although the original design envisioned perhaps one or two retired workers per 100 active workers contributing to the PAYGO system, the numbers have now increased to 12 retired workers per hundred active workers in the year 2010, globally. And, although some developing countries (such as India) still have old age dependency ratios of eight retirees per 100 workers, in other countries the ratio is as much as triple the world average—or more. For example, in Japan the number is close to 35 retirees per 100 workers, and in Germany, the birthplace of the state pension plan, the ratio is close to 30 per 100. In the year 2050, assuming current fertility ratios continue, Japan will be facing an astonishing 75 retirees per 100 workers; whereas Germany, Italy, and Spain will have almost 60 retirees to support for every 100 people in the labor force. For all these countries, there is a connection between their high projected future old-age dependency ratios and their low fertility rates: In Japan, the fertility rate is 1.2 lifetime births per woman; in Spain, it is 1.3; and in Germany, it is 1.4.[5] It is clear that for countries with PAYGO pensions, small families and few children can

---

5. Projections of worldwide dependency ratios are taken from *The 2009 Ageing Report* by the European Commission.

lead to problems.[6] For those of you who are wondering, the situation in the United States isn't as bleak, although it is certainly worrisome. In 2010, the old-age dependency ratio is close to 20 retirees per 100 workers, and it is expected to hit 35 by the year 2050. These are not European or Japanese numbers, partially because of the relatively higher U.S. fertility rate of 2.1. Furthermore, the U.S. Social Security system isn't as generous (it doesn't pay as much) as European or Japanese state pension plans, which is yet another reason that the United States has some time before it faces the PAYGO pension crisis unfolding in many other countries, although the United States will soon have to contend with this as well.

Interestingly, and more relevant to our discussion, when Chancellor Bismarck's pension scheme was introduced to the German Reichstag back in 1881, he emphasized that the motivation for his reforms was to preserve a sense of human dignity for the elderly and to prevent them from having to rely on charity. Perhaps the PAYGO pension system can be understood as the *revenge* of the elderly (Bismarck had just turned 66) and the infirm against the young and agile. In fact, to quote a recent German study, "Bismarck wanted the pension system as a substitute for the transfer mechanisms of the traditional family that had been destroyed by the industrial revolution, seeing it mainly as a means to avoid the neglect and mistreatment of old people by their children." The article continues that, "A PAYGO system may serve as *an enforcement device for ungrateful children*."[7]

Thwarted by Good Intentions

Although Bismarck had good intentions, the viability of his funding system has been called into question. When Bismarck picked the age of 70 as the age of retirement, life expectancy in Germany (at birth) was a mere 39 years. It was rare for people to reach the age of retirement, and even those who were lucky didn't live

---

6. See Beck, "A Slow-Burning Fuse," especially "Scrimp and Save: Pensions Will Have to Become Far Less Generous," and "Suffer the Little Children: Most of the Rich World is Short of Babies."
7. Emphasis added. Sinn, "The Pay-as-You Go Pension System as Fertility Insurance and an Enforcement Device."

very long after. Indeed, if the German retirement system had added as many years to the retirement age as have been added to overall life expectancy over the last century, the official retirement age would now stand at 95 years rather than 65![8] But now, as fertility rates drop and life expectancies continue to rise, and as the traditional age of retirement has actually decreased since Bismarck's initial proposal to 65, the sustainability of this model is increasingly uncertain. And so, perhaps when you think about the high cost of raising children, it's worth noting that your kids might be your (only) pensions given the current fiscal imbalances and structural deficits of most government pension plans such as U.S. Social Security. That is, investing in your kids' developing human capital might help reduce your own personal liabilities many years from now, in retirement.

What am I talking about?

Think back to the picture of the holistic personal balance sheet I presented in the Introduction, "Human Capital: Your Greatest Asset." On the left side are capital assets, and on the right side are liabilities. Some of these liabilities are *explicit*, such as the loans and debts I discussed in Chapter 3 ("How Much Debt Is Too Much and How Much Is Too Little?"), but many others are *implicit*. The birth of a child creates an immediate, implicit liability on the parents' holistic balance sheet in that she or he must be cared for, and this requires resources. This liability might explain why the net worth of families is lower, on average. But there is another hidden liability on your holistic balance sheet; one that your kids might actually be able to help you offset—the cost and debts that can accrue as you age. For example, people over the age of 65 spend about four times as much as those under 65 on health care, and a 1997 study found the average cost of nursing home care in the U.S. ranges from $36,000 to $80,000 per year.[9] I am going to suggest that in most (if not all) families with an above-average number of children—and yes, these families have

---

8. Liedtke, "From Bismarck's Pension Trap to the New Silver Workers of Tomorrow."

9. Health care costs for people under and over 65 are taken from Goldman and McGlynn, "U.S. Health Care." Estimates of national U.S. nursing home expenditures are drawn from data provided by the National Center for Health Statistics, 2000.

incurred above-average costs of child raising—parents are shielded from many of the costs of aging. In other words, your kids can function like pensions!

I am not just speculating (or hoping, since I do have four daughters). A number of recent studies by gerontologists and social workers have identified similar cost savings. Research from data in developing and developed countries alike suggests that a "statistically significant" portion of grown-up children (27 percent, in one U.S. study) transfer personal services and cash to their elderly parents, even in countries with the "most extensive pension and welfare systems."[10] However, it seems that although some children and grandchildren are their parent's pension plan, in some cases the situation is reversed, and the pension that was intended for the grandparent ends up in the pockets and bellies of the grandchildren. In fact, if the evidence from South Africa is instructive, this is true more so for girls than for boys, and for grandmothers more than grandfathers. According to researchers, female grandchildren living with grandmother state pension recipients saw improved health outcomes as a result of the pension income coming into the household. Yet oddly enough, when grandchildren lived with a grandfather, there was no change in the children's health.[11] Perhaps grandmothers use pension income to smooth consumption across the lives of their granddaughters as opposed to their own life.

So, here's the bottom line: The birth of a child is truly a milestone in your human life cycle, with importance on an order of magnitude that can't be quantified using dollars and cents. That said, like the other significant decisions in your life, there is a financial angle to having children that also can't be ignored. Indeed, the short- and medium-term costs of children can be enormous. For many people, children are thus a "luxury good" that must be rationed and budgeted for. And yet, as I have argued, the long-term implications on your personal balance sheet associated with having children might be contrary to conventional wisdom. Your teenager might eat you out of house and home

---

10. The discussion of transfers from grown-up children to elderly parents (or "children as pensions") is taken from Cigno, "How to Avoid a Pension Crisis: A Question of Intelligent System Design."

11. Duflo, "Grandmothers and Granddaughters."

today *but will help you smooth consumption tomorrow* as he cares for
you in later years, either by supporting you financially or by providing
goods and services that you'd otherwise need to purchase. After your
kids are born, your balance sheet needs to adjust to include both the
implicit immediate liabilities associated with raising a child, but also
the future implicit asset they represent for you. As a parent, you are,
once again, wealthier than you think. And that measure doesn't include
the cute dividends that having children can pay—that is, grandkids!

Now let's look at how marriage changes our approaches to financial risk. I'll focus on one population subset I find especially allur-
ing—Italian women.

Is Marriage a Safe Investment on the Balance Sheet?

A number of researchers around the world have documented that
women tend to have more conservative, that is, less risky, investment
portfolios than men, and that single females are less likely to invest in
risky assets such as stocks and equities, compared to females who are
married. The consensus from the research seems to be that women
have a higher degree of financial risk aversion and a lower tendency
to allocate their financial capital (and perhaps even human capital) to
risky endeavors than men do.

One of the most frequently referenced studies related to this phenomenon was conducted by two researchers at the University of Cali-
fornia and published under the provocative title "Boys Will Be
Boys."[12] This study provided ample evidence to argue that men are
more prone to what behavioral economists call *overconfidence* in
investing (which isn't good for anybody, actually). According to the
authors, this overconfidence leads men to needlessly trade more frequently than women, while investing their savings in a more hazardous manner. As a group, the researchers found that men were
trading more frequently and investing more riskily because they think
they have specialized skill or knowledge about investing, when in
fact—judging by their results in aggregate—they do not. As a result, in

---

12. See Barber and Odean.

the long run, men's portfolios (especially those of single men) actually earn less than female investors who are less prone to overconfidence. I'm sure that you might resonate with this particular explanation—in particular the women among you—but I believe there might be a deeper and perhaps more satisfying explanation for the "single, female, and safe" portfolio phenomenon. This alternative explanation comes from a recent study of the marital habits and investment decisions of Italian women, conducted by (Italian) researchers at the Institute for the Study of Labor (IZA) in Bonn.[13] Now, being married to a strong-minded Italian woman whose large family immigrated to Canada in the 1950s, let me admit at the outset that first, I have to be very careful about what I say here, and second, I'm clear that Italian women don't take *any* decisions lightly, especially decisions about marriage. They think strategically, and children and the family are the center of their universe. Indeed, as you will see, you can learn much from the financial acumen of Italian women!

Getting back to our study: researchers at the IZA used data from the Bank of Italy's survey of Household Income and Wealth, which is a detailed dataset similar in scope and purpose to the U.S. Survey of Consumer Finances, during the period 1989 to 2006. The authors presented evidence, consistent with the international evidence, that unmarried Italian women are the least likely to hold risky investment assets such as corporate stocks and common shares. Married women, in contrast, don't exhibit the same reluctance to assume investment risk.

The researchers found that in 1989, the first year for which they had data, single (Italian) females allocated almost 90 percent of their investable financial capital to safe assets and only negligible amounts to risky investments. In contrast, in the same year, married (Italian) females had closer to 85 percent in safe assets and a much larger fraction in risky investments. Although the reported differences might not appear substantial, these numbers are statistically significant and quite robust across more than 71,000 individual observations. Moreover, this variation in risky versus safe asset holdings could not be explained by age, income, wealth, or education. In other words, even

13. Bertocchi, Brunetti, and Torricelli, "Marriage and Other Risky Assets: A Portfolio Approach."

after separating the data into groups of people with equal education, equal wealth, equal income, and so on, the researchers observed the "single, female, and safe" phenomenon. So what happened? Could marriage have changed Italian women's risk tolerance or emboldened them to invest more like men? It seems that marriage enamors women...*to the stock market.*

The authors' explanation for this increased risk tolerance was not psychological, biological, or behavioral. Rather, they attributed this behavior to the intuitive concept of the *family balance sheet* and the value of human capital. In the authors' words, "Our hypothesis is that marriage may work as a sort of safe asset when women make portfolio decisions." In my words, women focus on the holistic balance sheet of the family unit and make investment decisions based on all sources of human capital. After they are married, their holistic balance sheet gains another source of stable income that then enables them to take on greater investment risk, even if their so-called personal risk tolerance remains unchanged.

Two Plus Two Equals a Very Safe Four

I will return to the impact of human capital on investment and portfolio considerations later in Chapter 8 ("Portfolio Construction: What Asset Class Do You Belong To?"), but for now, it's worth noting that just like for these Italian women, the entire family's human capital should ideally be taken into account in all household financial and investment decisions. Moreover, although human capital is the most valuable asset on the personal balance sheet, it is much safer to have two people each earning and generating their own wages, compared to only one individual earning double the wages. In this case, 50 plus 50 is definitely *safer than* 100, even though it might be *equal to* only 100. It seems that Italian women intuitively know this and base their financial decisions accordingly. In short, marriage enables them to take risks that would have been imprudent otherwise.

Now, this study of Italian women provides more than just another hypothesis or different explanation for observed gender and marital status behavior. The authors actually produce some clever evidence that backs up their "portfolio of marriage" theory. But first, some more Italian background, not about marriage, but about its opposite—divorce.

In Italy, divorce did not become legal until the mid-1970s. As you might imagine, the Roman Catholic Church tried hard to prevent the legalization of divorce by lobbying for various referendums when the legislation was introduced, but by 1974, it was (finally) possible to divorce in Italy. Initially couples could obtain a divorce only after five years of legal separation, but the (reported) divorce rate jumped from virtually zero in the early 1970s to almost 30 percent by the end of the decade. By 2006, the Italian divorce rate was approaching 50 percent.

The reason this is relevant to our study is that as divorce rates increase—all over the world, and not just in Italy—you would expect to see a gradual erosion of the perception of marriage as a safe asset. In other words, the observed difference between the financial capital allocations of (currently) married females and (currently) single females should weaken. And, in fact, that is exactly what our Italian authors observed over the 18 years of data. They conclude, "The differential behavior of single women has evolved over time, and this evolution, rather than being determined by exogenous [external] variations in risk attitudes, can be related to the increased incidence of divorce and the expansion of female labor market participation. Our results suggest that women's perception of marriage as a safe asset, as reflected by their portfolio choices, has been shaped by the transformation of the structure of the family and society." In other words, Italian women are no longer placing as much stock, literally, in marriage as a safe asset but are hedging their risk (of marriage breakdown) by increasingly investing like single women.

From my perspective, these findings fit quite nicely with my position that many of the decisions people face over their human life cycle, such as marriage and the possibility of divorce, are (at least partially) driven by holistic balance sheet and income smoothing considerations. That is, when you make milestone decisions, whether about kids or marriage (or divorce), you should always keep an eye on the financial angle.

Fiscally Fatal Attractions

Although Italian women display evidence of careful portfolio considerations when it comes to marriage, it seems that back in the United States the result is less conclusive. If you focus strictly on financial considerations, you find that some women consistently marry the wrong guy (and *vice versa*) according to an interesting study by researchers at Wharton Business School and Northwestern University.[14] In general, the consensus among researchers (and marriage counselors) is that when selecting marriage partners, both males and females tend to select people with comparable traits, similar values—and occasionally even the same name! This finding is consistent with the old saying that "birds of a feather, flock together" and is described in academic literature as *positive assortment* (the act of distributing things into classes or categories of the same type) as opposed to *complementarity* (relations between opposites).

However, when looking strictly at how attitudes toward finances play into how people choose mates, you don't find "birds of a feather, flock together" but exactly the opposite. Apparently, a disproportionate number of (what the researchers call) tightwads tend to marry (what the researcher call) spendthrifts. And, surprisingly, neither is very happy as a result.

The Wharton and Northwestern researchers surveyed close to a thousand people, almost half of whom were married, and asked them questions about their "emotional reactions" to spending. In particular, they were asked a variety of questions—with answers on a scale of one to seven—about whether the prospect of spending money made them *anxious, conflicted,* or *regretful*. Individuals reporting larger values (close to 7) were considered "tightwads," who generally spend less than they would ideally like to spend; whereas individuals with lower self-declared scores (close to 1) were considered "spendthrifts," who generally spend more than they would ideally like to spend. Next, these individuals were asked to report and quantify their spouse's emotional reactions to the prospect of spending money, using the same "spendthrift to tightwad" scale. Now, you might not consider this the best or only measure of emotional attitudes to spending versus saving, but it is a fair starting point. The survey was administered to both members of the couple, and it included standard questions that measure marital well-being by assessing the

---

14. Scott, Small, and Finkel, "Fatal (Fiscal) Attraction: Spendthrifts and Tightwads in Marriage."

extent to which partners are satisfied with the marriage, agree on important issues, and share interests. Finally, the researchers also posed questions that measured the extent to which money was a source of conflict in the marriage.

Birds of a Feather May Not Flock Together

The result from all these surveys and questions was indisputable and quite interesting. The correlation between tightwad/spendthrift scores of individuals and their spouses was negative and statistically significant. In other words, opposites are often attracted (or at least married) to each other. In the language of the researchers, *complementarity* as opposed to *positive assortment* is observed. Moreover, this bodes poorly for marriages because the same pairs scored quite low on the marital well-being scale.

Now, why there might be an "opposites attract" phenomena when it comes to fiscal prudence and financial attitudes is subject to some speculation, but the authors of the study suggest a rather peculiar reason: They blame it on a form of self-loathing. Bear with me here for a moment. In their words, "We find that the extent to which people are attracted to mates with opposing emotional reactions towards spending is significantly correlated with the extent to which they are dissatisfied with their own emotional reactions towards spending." The researchers actually replicated these results in a variety of other survey formats and questionnaires that corrected for some of the possible biases that might occur when people are asked to self-assess attitudes to money.

Although unmarried people claim in surveys that they would like and plan to select mates who share their emotional attitude toward spending and savings, to the extent that they *dislike* their relationship with spending, they tend to actually be attracted and actually marry people with *the exact opposite emotional attitude*. They might be attempting to correct for or influence the disliked aspect of the self with this mate choice—perhaps even to diversify the household's approach to spending (as one splurges, the other will show restraint). However, whatever their motivations were, this strategy did not lead to greater marital bliss; the research suggests that these differences in emotional attitudes toward spending and saving are actually associated with greater financial conflict and diminished well-being in marriage.

Either way, the results of the above study serve to remind us that although it might be optimal to think of the family unit as a diversifying source of human capital, which then allows you to better smooth consumption and practice (what I call) Long Division in a rational manner, there are many other psychological factors that can have an extraneous impact on the monetary milestones in your life. Perhaps diversification is good when it comes to financial capital, but not when it comes to emotional attitudes to money. In other words: Don't count on your spouse to bail you out of your attitude toward spending—or understand that if you do, your marriage might suffer as a result.

Summary: The Four Principles in Action

- At first glance, it seems that the act of MULTIPLICATION (by adding to your family) makes you poorer, by SUBTRACTING assets you now need to care for that child. But, in addition to all the other wonderful benefits from children, they also ADD to the holistic personal balance sheet. Accounting for children on your holistic personal balance sheet involves both subtraction (when they are young) and surprisingly enough, addition (when you are old).

- With the decreasing number of active workers available to support pensions for retired workers, the viability of state-sponsored pension plans is increasingly in question. One alternative source of pension-like income transfers is children. Perhaps people with large families already have this figured out—DIVIDING support for parents among many kids.

- Evidence from married Italian women—and anecdotally verified by many others—suggests that marriage can be viewed as a financially stabilizing event, enabling women to take on more investment risk than their single counterparts because two plus two salaries ADD up to a safer income stream.

- Speaking of marriage, it seems that self-loathing tightwads and spendthrifts are often married to one another. However, these relationship matches tend to SUBTRACT from marital happiness over time.

You see. Everything boils down to four basic arithmetic operations!

5

Government Tax Authorities: Partners, Adversaries, or Bazaar Merchants?

In late 1994, just around the festive Christmas and New Year's time of year, the State of Minnesota carried out what can be described only as a cruel experiment on its citizens. When I tell this story to my students, they often shudder and some even groan aloud. I like to start my lecture (and now this chapter) with the story of this infamous experiment because it can teach us quite a bit about the most unpleasant, reoccurring financial milestone in everyone's life: April 15, which is the deadline for filing taxes in the United States.[1] Here's what happened in Minnesota. Approximately 47,000 taxpayers who filed their (1993) tax returns properly and on time were chosen at random in April 1994 by the Commissioner of Revenue for an "experimental treatment" in anticipation of the next tax filing season. From this large group, one subgroup received a generic letter reminding them to file their taxes honestly and on time. Another subgroup was informed they had been selected to access special assistance in compiling their federal tax returns by calling a free help line. Finally, about 2,000 people were informed by the commissioner, in writing, that the tax returns they were about to file would be *closely examined* by the Department of Revenue. Their names had been randomly generated, and their selection for this subgroup had nothing to do with (and was not motivated by) their behavior or compliance in the previous year. Each one of these 2,000 people was told in advance that they would be audited no matter what they did, who they were, and how they completed their tax returns. Under

---

1. In Canada, the yearly deadline is April 30.

normal circumstances, only 1 percent of returns are audited by the tax authorities. But this group was given the "benefit" of being warned to cross every "t" and dot every "i" in their upcoming tax return. What a wonderful Christmas card!

So what was this experiment about? The tax authorities wanted to see how, if at all, this advance notice would alter the behavior and reported income, deductions, and tax liabilities of this particular "treatment group" relative to previous years and relative to similar individuals who did not receive the advance warning letter. The authorities (claimed that they) didn't want to torture these 2,000 people but simply wanted to use the experimental results in an attempt to measure the extent of tax evasion in Minnesota.

The subsequent behavior of this rather unlucky group of taxpayers is the focus of the next few pages and the impetus for our discussion of the most unpleasant money milestone of all: income taxes. How would *you* alter your behavior if you got such an advance notice, instead of facing the usual 1 percent chance of an audit? Would you be more cautious; claim fewer deductions; and make sure to report every penny? Alternatively, would you behave the same as you did last year? (Be honest now.) The results of this particular experiment will surprise you.

Before I report on the results, here are a few more relevant details about the experiment. The Department of Revenue in Minnesota segmented this "lucky" group of 2,000 people into three broad groups based on their reported 1993 adjusted gross income (AGI). The first group with a reported AGI of less than $10,000 was labeled the *low-income* group. The *middle-income* group had an AGI between $10,000 and $100,000, and the *high-income* group included anybody with an AGI greater than $100,000. Finally, each person, regardless of their AGI, was identified as either having a *high opportunity to evade* taxes or a *low opportunity* to evade taxes, based on whether the bulk of their income came from a sole proprietorship (that is, small business income) versus employment income from which taxes are automatically deducted at source. So, to recap, six subgroups were created in total: three categories of income and two categories around the opportunity to evade.

By the way, all this information was publicly disclosed and published (a few years after the experiment) by a number of researchers involved in the project, including economics professors at the National Bureau of Economic Research (NBER), which is the primary source for the preceding numbers and the conclusions.[2] The NBER economists analyzed the results of the experiment in conjunction with the staff from the Minnesota Department of Revenue, and their published paper offers some novel insights into the magnitude of tax evasion and the behavior of individuals facing a tax audit.

How Do Taxpayers Behave if "Big Brother" Is Watching?

On to the results: First, as you might have suspected, the treatment group reported more income and paid more taxes relative to the control group (taxpayers who were not warned) and relative to the same group's taxes for the previous year (adjusted for economic factors such as inflation). Overall, it seems the warning scared them and they behaved more honestly, especially those who had a natural (high) opportunity to evade. But the results were far from uniform, and in some cases, surprisingly, the exact opposite result occurred.

How so? Well, the low-income and medium-income groups who received the warning increased the federal taxable income they declared relative both to previous years and to the random group who did not get advance warning. This increased reported income effect was even more pronounced among those who were classified as having a higher opportunity to evade taxes. That is, they might have cut some corners in previous years and were apparently much more careful in a year in which they knew their returns would be scrutinized carefully.

But, oddly enough, and this is the surprising part of the study, the high income group actually reported *lower* federal taxable income, paid less federal tax, and reported lower Minnesota state liabilities. This is seemingly quite odd. Why would their results differ from the other groups?

---

2. Blumenthal, Christian, and Slemrod, "The Determinants of Income Tax Compliance."

To drill down further: Among the group of taxpayers who owned small businesses and sole proprietorships and received nonemployment income, the wealthier (those who had adjusted gross income greater than $100,000) group reported average federal taxable income of $143,000 for tax year 1994, compared to $176,000 in the prior year. Let me repeat: The people in this group were warned in advance that they would be audited, and they still declared a lower income than the previous year—almost $20,000 lower compared to the unwarned "control" groups who reported an average income of $163,000 *and fully $33,000 less than they themselves reported the previous year.* This difference was statistically significant (with a high level of confidence) and thus was extremely unlikely to be the result of chance.

Treat Your Tax Filing Like a Trip to the Bazaar

Would *you* be more aggressive when filing your tax returns if you were certain of an audit? This seems like a perverse result. This is not just a handful of people who behaved this way. And unfortunately, it was impossible to ask the taxpayers why they behaved more aggressively—they surely wouldn't admit it—or why their behavior differed so remarkably from the low- and medium-income earners.

Here is the explanation that has been proposed to explain this behavior, which actually leads to one of the main messages of this chapter. In the words of the NBER economists and authors of the definitive study of the experiment, "We have come up with two possible explanations.... The first is that the audit notice letter induced taxpayers to seek out professional tax advisors who, among other things, uncovered legitimate ways to reduce taxable income that the taxpayer had previously been unaware of." They continued to say, "The second...relies on the idea that, even upon audit, the 'true' tax liability is not ascertainable. The tax liability ultimately paid depends on, among other things, a *process of negotiation* between the taxpayer and the [tax authorities]."[3] In other words, the wealthier folks essentially

---

3. Pages 20-21. Emphasis added.

viewed their inevitable date with the tax inspector like experienced tourists visiting an outdoor Moroccan bazaar. The tourist wants to buy an exotic carpet or antique vase at the lowest possible price, and the vendor wants to extract the highest possible selling price. The tourist starts with a ridiculously low and actually insulting bid for the item, which is more often than not followed by a ridiculously high offer from the vendor. This haggling process continues back and forth over a number of bargaining rounds until some equilibrium point is reached between the tourist's initial bid and the vendor's initial offer. And so, what is the true price of the carpet or vase? Who knows? All that is known is what this particular haggling session ended with as an agreed-upon price. Tomorrow, later this afternoon, or next week, the same item will be sold for a completely different price depending on the next tourist's bargaining stamina and negotiating appetite and ability. This is what the researchers were saying: The true amount of tax owing is not fixed but is arrived at through the process of negotiation.

Thus, perhaps in contrast to a classical view of the tax code and regulations as setting out fixed and unvarying obligations, there actually isn't a universal and rigid agreed-upon measure of undisputable personal tax liability. Maybe our tax liabilities are subjective and negotiable, especially for those in the very high-income (and self-employed) groups that have many more opportunities to haggle. Get the right tax accountant or tax lawyer on your side of the stand and your visit to the Moroccan bazaar will turn out differently. Of course, at relatively low levels of income and in one-dimensional situations in which your only income comes from an employer from which taxes have already been withheld by the time you get your pay, your freedom to negotiate is down to virtually zero. This is why the Minnesotans with income less than $100,000 who now faced a certain audit were so much more careful and declared greater relative income. But at higher and more complex levels, it becomes a game between you and the tax authorities. In fact, perhaps even at lower levels one should adopt a *souk*-like attitude to taxes.

Hopefully you can (now) see why the results from the experiment have direct implications to anyone who faces an income tax milestone. I am obviously not advocating tax evasion or avoidance. I am advocating extreme tax awareness, tax vigilance, and tax efficiency.

Tax Authorities as Lifetime Partners in Your Business

I like to think about the tax authorities and the government as a lifetime business partner who shares in a fraction of all your business gains, and shares or subsidizes your business losses. This relationship is dynamic and universal. You might not like your partner very much, and you might feel that you got a raw deal when you signed the partnership contract or that your partner is too aggressive at times, but the bottom line is *you have a lifetime partner.* If you earn $100, you must share the appropriate sum with your business partner, but if you lose $100, the business partner will subsidize a portion of the loss. And so, just as your partner keeps a close eye on your activities to make sure you pay your fair share of the agreement, you must ensure that your partner is not taking too much. Furthermore, each financial decision you make and money milestone you face should be considered in terms of how it influences your share of the partnership income. Taxes are not something you should think about once per year and treat like the inevitable and indisputable cost of the postage stamp you use to send in the return. Rather, the reality of taxes should form an ever-present factor in every financial decision you make. Ask yourself, always; *what are the tax implications of this money milestone?*

Indeed, according to Internal Revenue Service estimates quoted in the same study, although 60 percent of middle-income taxpayers understated their true tax liability and only 26 percent reported it correctly, a full 14 percent of taxpayers *overstated* their tax liability. In other words, they paid more than they had to. This can be viewed only as sheer sloppiness or laziness on the part of taxpayers. The message here is that you can legally control your tax liability by much more than you think. Don't be passive. Be proactive.

Tax Lessons from Uruguay (a Beautiful Little Country in South America)

Over the last few years, I have spent some time in the city of Montevideo, Uruguay, where I teach a short course at the local university on the topic of financial planning and wealth management.

Teaching this one-week course has been a revelation for both the students and for me. They are fascinated by how people deal with money milestones in North America, and I am equally fascinated by what they teach me about how things work in South America.

One of the rather surprising things I learned about financial planning in Uruguay is that salaries, wages, and income tend to be reported and discussed on an after-tax as opposed to pre-tax basis. (This is true in Argentina and Brazil as well.) In other words, if you happen to be asked (and you are willing to divulge) how much you earn, the number you give is likely to be in after-tax dollars. This is not just some odd habit or convention. When you get a job offer and you are told that your salary is 100,000 pesos, the employer means net to you, after withholding, after deductions, and after taxes. That's the number on the check and deposited into your bank account as your take-home pay. Now compare this to North America. When I got my first part-time summer job (back in New York City in the 1980s), I was shocked to get my first paycheck. The number was nothing near what had been promised in my employment contract! Then, after a few minutes, it hit me. Taxes were owed and were being deducted at source. The salary I had been promised was on a pretax basis. On an after-tax basis (that is, the dollars I could actually consume), the numbers were 30 percent lower. Moreover, in some jurisdictions and at higher income levels, the gross versus net can hit 50 percent.

When I tell my South American students that you can be promised and guaranteed $100,000 in salary, but never really get that (ever) because of taxes, they chuckle at the naiveté of Americans and Canadians who are fooled by pretax numbers. In fact, they can't help but wonder why anybody bothers to quote, reference, or cite on anything but an after-tax basis. I think there is much to learn from these Uruguayans. It's time to focus much closer attention on the after-tax returns, after-tax income, and the general tax efficiency of our investments and our personal income statement. That is: Keep an eye on your business partner throughout the entire year, not just in April.

Another Puzzle: People Prefer Big Tax Refunds

While on the topic of puzzling behavior when it comes to income taxes, I am always amused to see the large number of hands that go up when I ask the students in my class: *Who here would like to get a large tax refund after you file your income taxes this year?* As you might expect, most students say yes, and the question even appears like a "no-brainer" to many. In fact, you too might raise your hand and want to get a refund. According to the Internal Revenue Service, approximately 75 percent of tax filers get a refund check from the government, and the average size of the check is around $2,500. In Canada, the numbers are somewhat smaller, and the average refund is approximately $1,400 Canadian dollars.

But when you think about it carefully and rationally, you don't really want a refund. You want to file your taxes and either owe little or perhaps get a small refund. In fact, if you (consistently) get a large refund, you have not been planning your financial affairs efficiently; your employer is deducting too much tax at the source, and you should do something about it. Economists and tax specialists have a name for this: *over-withholding*, which is when taxpayers remit more in tax payments over the course of the tax year than they actually owe in tax by the end of the tax year. Let me be clear about this: With over-withholding you are giving an interest-free loan to the government during the entire year, and you aren't compensated nor do you get any brownie points for this.

However, you aren't required to do this: You have a choice. For example, in the U.S., tax filers can take advantage of the advanced Earned Income Tax Credit (EITC), and in Canada taxpayers can file forms TD1 and T12131 (requesting that tax credits and deductions be taken into account on your withholdings throughout the year, as opposed to waiting for tax filing time).

It is ironic that although people get upset at the size of their paycheck at the end of the month, few take simple steps to do anything about it. Even when people are told explicitly about their ability to reduce withholding taxes, and get more money today, the vast majority simply chose not to. Honestly. I didn't make this up. When you think about it, getting a lump sum and large refund after you file your tax returns, and getting a smaller-than-required paycheck during the year, violates the number one axiom of money milestones: Long Division. Getting a large payment later instead of many smaller earlier ones is the exact opposite of consumption smoothing.

According to two economists at the University of Michigan and the Federal Reserve Board, the puzzling preference for over-withholding is especially prevalent among individuals with low and moderate incomes.[4] These economists designed and helped administer a questionnaire that they sent to more than a thousand such households, partially to understand why they were engaging in this seemingly irrational behavior. The authors of this study (and their staff) interviewed more than 1,000 households in the Detroit metropolitan area, where the median income is approximately $49,000 per year. They were careful to skew their sampling toward lower and middle-income families. Participants were asked whether they received a tax refund (80 percent of those who filed said yes), whether they used a tax preparer to help them file the returns (66 percent had), and whether they received an advance against their refund (a *refund anticipation loan*, which can be quite costly in terms of interest rates).

However, here is where it is puzzling. Respondents were asked specifically if they would like to get "a paycheck that is $100 larger each month than your current one, with a tax refund that is $1,200 smaller." This question was reversed, and the same group was also asked if they would rather get "a paycheck that was $100 smaller each month, with a tax refund that is $1,200 larger at the end of the year." No matter how the question was phrased, it seems that over one-third of the group would rather have more withheld in exchange for a bigger refund—that actually has a lower present discounted value. More than half the participants were happy with the status quo (that is, their smaller paycheck and larger refund), and less than 20 percent of the group "woke up" to the financial advantage and stated that yes, they actually would like less withheld and a smaller refund.

The authors were struck by the lack of rationality in all this and not just because it violates some theory of how people are supposed

---

4. Barr and Dokko, *Paying to Save*.

to behave. They found that a large majority of low and middle income taxpayers would prefer to over-withhold and pay more taxes than needed so that they could get a refund at tax filling time. In other words, "many of [these] individuals would like to use the federal with-holding system in effect to save in a temporarily illiquid manner." They note that, in contrast to peoples' observed behavior, "many [low- and middle-income people] would benefit from having their refund distributed evenly throughout the year, particularly in light of the credit constraints and high cost borrowing opportunities available to this group." The authors ultimately conclude by saying "that tax filers want to over-withhold means they are willing to pay in order to save." That is, their study found that people with less money and a clear identified need for the tax return funds do not take advantage of opportunities to put that (their!) money in their pocket earlier—and they actually, in effect, pay the government for the use of their money before it is refunded to them—both in foregone interest and because a high proportion of the people surveyed take out refund anticipation loans and "pay a non-trivial fee to a tax preparer, in order to expedite the receipt of a tax refund."

In the end, the researchers determined that this phenomena falls outside the realm of rational behavior and could be explained only as suggesting that tax filers "seek a pre-commitment device against the tendency to over-consume." That is, the households were ensuring they didn't overspend during the year, by allowing their "business partner" to keep more than the partner's share of income as a kind of informal loan until tax time. Effective? Maybe. Irrational? For sure.

The After-Tax Return Matters

Wealthier readers of this book, for whom an early versus later refund of a mere thousand or so dollars isn't very exciting, should note that similar behavior can be observed with much greater sums of money. And, at those levels, suboptimal behavior can cost tens of thousands of dollars. One of the best examples of this is related to the sale, promotion, and advertising of mutual fund investment returns.

First, let me give some refresher background on investments and taxes. When you buy a stock, bond, or any other investment, you don't have to worry about paying any capital gains (and hence income) taxes until you sell the investment at a profit. In between the purchase and sale, the only taxes you have to concern yourself with are possible interest (on bonds) and dividends (on stocks) that you might receive during the holding period. These are taxable in the year in which you receive them.

Now let's think about a typical mutual fund that invests in a combination of (many) stocks and (many) bonds. If the manager of the mutual fund holds on to those stocks and bonds—and doesn't buy and sell them very often—then the only taxes you, as a fund holder, must worry about are the same dividend payments and interest income that are passed through to you.

On the other hand, if the fund manager engages in frequent trading of the investments, and turns over the stocks and bonds on a regular basis, you might find yourself paying capital gains on profits made by the manager, even though you bought and held the mutual fund itself. Therefore, when a mutual fund manager who buys and sells various stocks and bonds advertises that it earned 10 percent (for example) in a given year, there are three quite different possibilities for how this 10 percent was obtained:

- The entire 10 percent might be due to interest or dividends received, or both, even if the underlying securities themselves didn't increase in value.
- Alternatively, the stocks and bonds in the fund might have increased in value without being sold, and in addition, they earned some dividends and interest.
- Finally, the return might result from the investments themselves being sold for a profit.

All three options and any combination of these options can lead to the 10 percent. Now, this whole discussion might seem rather academic. After all, who cares how the 10 percent came about, as long as it's 10 percent? But from a tax point of view, how the return was derived can make an enormous difference. If the bulk of the gains came from "realized gains" (when a security is sold after having appreciated in price), you, as the mutual fund shareholder, will be liable for much more in taxes than if the gains were unrealized. Typically, mutual fund shareholders will be informed at the end of the tax year (by the company, your broker, or your advisor) exactly how much is taxable and how much is deferred.

Now, here is where this gets interesting. When you go into a local bank, credit union, or savings and loan association and are told that the interest rate on a one-year deposit is 5 percent, this obviously means that a $100 investment will grow to $105 by the end of the year. But remember, if these funds are sitting outside of a tax shelter like an IRA (or RRSP in Canada) or 401(k) plan, the $5 gain will be taxable. So, really, you don't get $5 on the $100 investment; you don't really get 5 percent. Yet, the bank can advertise 5 percent as the interest rate. The same thing applies to mutual funds. They can advertise that a fund earned 10 percent last year, but this is only on a pretax basis. On an after-tax basis this number can be as low as 5 percent depending on how much of the gains within the fund were realized versus unrealized.[5] Moreover, when investment fund companies advertise that their funds beat 95 percent of all other funds, or that Fund A was better than Fund B, all this is only on a pretax basis (and is actually applicable only to people who don't pay taxes).

Reversals of Fortune

In fact, a very intriguing (and early) study by two Stanford University economists, published by the National Bureau of Economic Research in 1993, examined the performance and growth of U.S. mutual funds during the 1963–1992 period on both a pretax and after-tax basis.[6] They calculated and compared the return that a hypothetical taxable investor would receive in each of these funds. They then arrived at the rather surprising result that "the differences between the relative ranking of funds on a before and after-tax basis

---

5. Recently the Securities and Exchange Commission (SEC) in the United States has imposed disclosure guidelines on mutual funds for reporting after-tax returns. The SEC requires mutual funds to disclose after-tax returns for one-, five- and ten-year periods in prospectuses and fund profiles prepared after February 15, 2002. After-tax returns must be calculated using the highest individual federal income tax rate. In Canada, this is not the case, and this disclosure is not provided by the companies.

6. Dickson and Shoven, "Ranking Mutual Funds on an After-Tax Basis."

are dramatic, especially for middle and high income investors. For example, one fund that ranks in the 19th percentile on a pretax basis ranks in the 61st percentile for an upper income taxable investor." This means that a fund that seemingly performed worse than fully 81 percent of its peers when viewed on a pre-tax basis rose to beat out 61 percent of those peers when the after-tax return is considered.

These types of result are not limited to U.S. mutual funds. In fact, partially inspired by the previously mentioned study, together with some colleagues, I conducted a similar study in Canada using Canadian mutual funds. The study was published in the *Canadian Tax Journal*, and the results were similar to the United States.[7] We examined ten years' worth of investment returns from 343 equity and balanced mutual funds managed by Canadian companies. Overall, we found that the ranking of mutual funds on a pretax basis is significantly different from their ranking on an after-tax basis. Moreover, two different funds that had relatively similar performance on a pretax basis had a 46 percent chance their ranking was reversed on an after-tax basis. We also found that mutual funds that reported top quartile (top 25 percent) performance on a pretax basis often had miserable (bottom quartile) performance on an after-tax basis. Finally, for someone in the highest marginal tax bracket, the average mutual fund lost approximately 135 basis points to taxes on fund distributions.

Over time, the cost of inefficient income tax management can wipe out any investment gains beyond low-turnover index funds. In other words, you can hire a brilliant manager to buy and sell stocks for you, and they might outsmart the overall market by a few percentage points each year. But, if that entire extra return, which the professional investment managers have christened using the Greek symbol *alpha*, comes from excessive buying and selling, you might end up worse off after tax. This point was made succinctly in a lovely article that was written by two well-known money managers in 1993 and published in the *Journal of Portfolio Management*, appropriately called "Is Your Alpha Big Enough to Cover Its Taxes?"[8] In contrast to

---

7. Mawani, Milevsky, and Panyagometh, "The Impact of Personal Income Taxes on Returns and Rankings of Canadian Equity Mutual Funds."
8. Jeffrey and Arnott.

the low and medium income taxpayers from Detroit I previously mentioned, who enjoyed the perverse idea of withholding large chunks of their paycheck, the wealthy are most likely to own mutual funds outside of a retirement tax shelter. They are the ones vulnerable to mutual fund ranking reversals and large tax bills from inefficient tax management. They might be losing far more compared to the inefficiency of waiting a year to get a few thousand dollars in tax refunds, and they have the most to gain by paying attention to after-tax returns.

Bottom Line: Get Tax Savvy

A recent study undertaken by economists at Baylor University, with results published in the *Journal of Wealth Management* in 2004, serves to remind us that income taxes can be large hidden liabilities on our holistic personal balance sheet.[9] Individuals with investments inside tax shelters such as IRA and 401(k) accounts might think they do not have to worry about the tax efficiency of their investments, because all gains are tax deferred and all funds withdrawn from these accounts are taxable as ordinary income. This is true to a point, but it doesn't imply that they can forget about tax implications completely. The future taxes that will be due on all withdrawals should be properly placed on the right side of the balance sheet. Your partner—the I.R.S. in the United States and the Canada Revenue Agency in Canada—actually owns close to 50 percent of the account. If you will be placing the value of human capital on the balance sheet and treating it as an asset (which I hope you do), *don't forget to include the value of all the taxes you will have to pay one day in the future on those left-hand tax-sheltered accounts.* Any comprehensive asset allocation decisions should consider this liability.

So, for example, imagine you have $100,000 (tax-sheltered) inside an IRA, invested entirely in government bonds, and $100,000 (taxable) invested entirely in stocks. You might think that you have $200,000 in net financial capital of which 50 percent is stocks and 50 percent is bonds; a perfectly balanced portfolio. Alas,

---

9. Reichenstein, "Tax-Aware Investing."

you would be wrong on two counts. First, if you are in the 40-percent tax bracket (just to keep things simple), your true (net) financial capital is only $160,000, because $40,000 of the money in the IRA belongs to your partner, the tax authority. This is not a hypothetical liability in the distant future: It belongs to them today. Second, of the $160,000 that is yours, approximately 62.5 percent is invested in stocks and 37.5 percent is invested in bonds. You have more equity than you think, and you might want to lighten up on the risk.

It might take time to get used to this way of thinking, but it is perfectly consistent with the overall approach I have taken during the entire book. To help you out, I've created a calculator at www.qwema.ca that enables you to divide your assets to take into account the amount you owe your "permanent business partner," the tax authority. And I've included a calculator that can help you calculate the tax implications of investing in tax-paid or tax-deferred accounts—IRAs versus Roth IRAs in the United States and Tax-Free Savings Accounts versus RRSPs in Canada. And, finally, I'll talk more about asset allocation and how human capital affects the mix later in Chapter 8 ("Portfolio Construction: What Asset Class Do You Belong To?"), but hopefully you get the main idea here.

Bottom line, from now on, please, next time anybody quotes an investment return, interest rate, salary or wage, ask yourself—and him or her—*what does this imply on an after-tax tax basis?* Make sure your perpetual tax partner doesn't get more than their fair share of your hard-earned cash. This money milestone is one that you should pay attention to on a daily basis.

Summary: The Four Principles in Action

- The best way to think about the tax authorities (that is, the government) is as a permanent business partner with whom you DIVIDE all your gains and losses. They own part of your human capital and part of your financial capital. Get used to it and start thinking strategically!

- In many countries, such as South America, people are much more aware of post- versus pre-tax cash flows and tend to discuss financial matters in true consumable dollars. In other words, these cultures are careful to SUBTRACT income taxes up front as opposed to at year end, when taxes are due and payable.

- Many Americans and Canadians are apparently willing to share more of their fair share of income with the tax authorities throughout the year, and then wait to get a large refund when they file their taxes. This preference is somewhat irrational and certainly violates one of the main ideas within strategic money milestone management, which is Long DIVISION.

- After-tax returns can matter even more for people holding unregistered investment accounts. Two mutual funds (or any investment) with the same before-tax returns can have different after-tax returns depending on how those returns were derived, and these effects can be MULTIPLIED from year to year. The phenomena of "ranking reversal" and large tax bills from inefficient tax management can SUBTRACT years of investment gains!

6

Can You Eat Your House or Will It Ever Pay Dividends?

You recall from our previous discussion (in the Introduction, "Human Capital: Your Greatest Asset") that for most people during most of our lives, human capital is the most valuable asset on our personal balance sheets. But have you ever thought about what asset is next in line—what your *second*-most-valuable asset is? It probably won't surprise you to learn that for homeowners, this spot is occupied by their personal residence. According to the Survey of Consumer Finances (SCF), their personal residence represented fully 85 percent of homeowners' financial net worth in 2007. For the general population under the age of 35 (not limited to homeowners), homes represented fully 220 percent of their net worth (and because this statistic includes all people, not just homeowners, it probably *understates* the mortgage debt held by under-35 homeowners). For people over 65, homes represented between 34 percent and 40 percent of their financial net worth.

These are big numbers, and they've been getting bigger over time.[1] Over the last two decades, housing has become a much larger portion of the personal balance sheet. In 1989, the average balance sheet (not including human capital) for homeowners had about 70 percent allocated to housing, which is 15 percent less than in the year 2007—that shift from 70 percent to 85 percent represents a significant

---

1. In Canada, the median mortgage amount for a principal residence jumped from $79,490 to $93,000 between 1999 and 2005 (in constant 2005 dollars), and the proportion of the personal balance sheet occupied by the primary residence increased from 36.3 percent to 38.6 percent over the same period. See Statistics Canada, *The Wealth of Canadians*.

increase in the proportion of assets allocated to housing over the last 20 years. In this chapter, you see the impact of changing allocations to housing on the personal balance sheets of Americans and the surprising impact that *social capital*——not human or financial capital—can make on your financial fortunes.

Floating Debt Obligations and Sinking Values

One of the impacts of the shift of financial capital allocations to the personal residence has been that our financial fortunes now increasingly fluctuate in lockstep with the value of housing. As discussed in Chapter 3 ("How Much Debt Is Too Much and How Much Is Too Little?"), the 2007 Survey of Consumer Finances reports that 46 percent of U.S. households have a mortgage on their principal residence. The average balance, in 2009 dollars, is about $153,000. But according to the website Moody'sEconomy.com, by mid-2009 a quarter of homeowners with mortgages were estimated to have mortgage loans that exceed the value of their house.[2] In other words, more than 10 million American households have negative real estate equity, or what has become known colloquially as being *upside down* or *underwater* on your mortgage loan.

Table 6.1 shows this in stark terms, as it provides some data on the change in housing values for some regions over the four years from December 2004 to December 2008, using data from the S&P/Case-Shiller Home Price Index.

But notwithstanding the significant size and impact of the real estate market, and its rise or fall in any given period, it's important to understand that a house—whether financed with a large, adjustable rate mortgage or a small, fixed rate mortgage—contains aspects of both *investment* and *consumption*.

It is difficult to forecast—in mid-2009—if and when these indices and regions will improve, or what these numbers will look like in

---

2. As quoted in Streitfeld, "The Pain of Selling a Home for Less Than the Loan."

TABLE 6.1 Is Your House an Investment or Consumption?: S&P/Case-Shiller Home Price Indices December 2004 to December 2008

Region	% Change
Chicago	-7.9%
Las Vegas	-36.7%
New York	-0.9%
Detroit	-34.3%
Seattle	15.6%
Minneapolis	-20.9%
Composite-10 index	-15.28%

2010/2011, but the fact remains that housing can decline in value, and for prolonged periods. It is definitely not a risk-free investment.

This distinction is basic, and it will not come as a surprise to anyone reading this book. And yet, it seems to me that this back-to-basics element of the housing money milestone has gotten downplayed in the discussions of housing over the past few years, which have focused on housing as an investment—whether "good" (when housing values are rising) or "bad" (when values are falling).

Back to the Holistic Balance Sheet

Let's go back to basics and think about what happens to your holistic personal balance sheet when you buy a house. Most people finance the purchase of a home with debt, that is, a mortgage. In the good old (prudent) days, new home buyers would put down 20 percent of the value of the house and finance the remaining cost of the house with a long-term 25- or 30-year fixed rate mortgage. Recently, people typically make a down payment of 2 percent or 1 percent or perhaps even zero, and finance the majority of the house with (volatile) floating rate debt that might take up to a century to pay off in full. In fact, according to the most recent U.S. Housing Survey, out of 70.2 million households, 9.4 percent reported purchasing their home with a zero downpayment; and of those who moved to a different home within the past year, 16.9 percent reported not having a down payment. These ratios increased considerably within the previous 10 years: in 1997, they were 6.1 percent and 5.71 percent, respectively.[3] At first glance, when you buy a house for, say, $500,000, you are increasing the left side of your personal balance sheet (your assets) by $500,000 dollars. If you used $50,000 as a downpayment, which came from your own assets, the increase in assets was only $450,000.

On the right side of the personal balance sheet, you had to finance the purchase of this house with debt, so if you made a 10 percent down payment and financed the other $450,000, your liabilities have increased by $450,000 in total. *The important thing to remember is that the equity on your personal balance sheet has not changed.* You have $450,000 more in assets and $450,000 more in liabilities—and you've converted financial capital into a down payment.

Now let's examine what your personal balance sheet will look like in five years, ignoring human capital considerations. If you have been carefully paying down your mortgage debt, perhaps the remaining liabilities have been reduced to $400,000. And, even if housing prices have not increased at all, you have created $50,000 more in equity in your home, for total equity of $100,000. (This is the original downpayment of $50,000 plus the $50,000 in total payments over the last five years.)

So far, so good. But now let's imagine that housing prices fell by 20 percent over that same five-year period. This isn't inconceivable—and is exactly what just happened in many regions of the United States over the last five years, as shown in Table 6.1. In that case, a 20 percent drop in the value of a $500,000 house leaves you with a balance sheet asset of $400,000. This is exactly what you owe in debt (mortgage) on the house, and you have no equity. The $50,000 you originally invested in the house is gone, and all the payments you have made in the last five years could essentially be considered rent. You are no further ahead now, financially, than you were five years ago. *All you did was consume housing.*

---

3. Data taken from the American Housing Survey, conducted by Bureau of the Census for the Department of Housing and Urban Development.

Let's explore that notion of consuming housing a little further. When you buy a house, you can think of a portion of the money you spent as creating additional and potential financial capital (an *investment*, in the world of financial capital). However, another fraction can be viewed as a prepayment of your future liabilities, namely your need for shelter. In other words, think of the money you spent on a house as partially going toward a mutual fund (an investment) and partly going toward a large supply of milk, eggs, cheese, and other household staples (things you consume).

The reality is that housing fulfills a need: your need for shelter. This is an implicit liability on your personal balance sheet. By purchasing a house you are pre-paying that liability in advance. Think of it like a pre-paid phone card, but for rent and for the rest of your life. According to this line of thinking, the $450,000 mortgage doesn't quite increase your total liabilities by $450,000 because you have reduced your implicit housing liability. What all this implies is that housing is part consumption (to defuse your implicit shelter liabilities) and part investment, and you should keep both of these dimensions in mind when you consider the housing money milestone.

My Strong Bias: Many Homeowners Should Have Rented

So, where does this leave us in terms of practical housing advice? For one, I think that a large proportion of individuals within the population should not own a house, or they should at least push off the purchase as long as possible, and instead rent. Anyone that followed this advice in the U.S. over the last few years, possibly the last few decades, *would be much better off today*. This is not just me being preachy or dispensing with advice that—with hindsight—proves correct. If you actually go back to one of the first principles I discuss in this book, namely Long Division and the spreading of resources over time, you can arrive at the same conclusion, but the reason is not as simple as you might think. It isn't because housing is a "bad investment" or has performed poorly relative to other asset classes. Instead, it relates to the investment characteristics of your human capital when you are young and as you age.

In a number of recent studies, a variety of mathematical economists have developed a control theory model to derive the optimal or rational approach to housing over the life cycle.[4] (I discussed Dynamic Control Theory in the Introduction.) You can think of their research as exploring how Mr. Spock (from *Star Trek*), who knows all the odds and can act completely logically, would behave. According to these researchers, most "typical" people under the age of 40 shouldn't own a house but should rent, instead. But again, this isn't recommended for the reasons you might think. Here's the Spock argument against home ownership early in life: When you are young the vast majority of your true wealth is locked up in human capital, which is illiquid, nondiversified, and definitely nontradable. It therefore makes little sense to invest yet another substantial amount of total wealth in yet another illiquid and nondiversifiable item like a house.

Sure, if you could buy a house that has a bedroom in New York City, a bathroom in Los Angeles, and a kitchen in Chicago and perhaps a garage in Las Vegas, yes, your home would be diversified. Buying a house as an investment has strong similarities to someone being convinced that stocks are good investment in the "long run," but they decide to buy only one stock for their portfolio. I don't care how reliable that one stock is, or how large are the dividends, that stock portfolio is not diversified. The same goes for housing.

In addition, when you are young, your human capital and hence your total wealth is sensitive to the evolution of your wages and income over time. These two factors tend to decline in a recession and bad economic times, *just like housing*. In other words, there is a good chance that if your job wages take a hit, so will your real estate. I will actually touch upon this concept again in Chapter 8 ("Portfolio Construction: What Asset Class Do You Belong To?"), when I discuss the interaction between your future wages versus stocks, bonds, and other investments. For now, it is simply worth pointing out that if your wages are sensitive to economic conditions; it makes little sense to exposure a large fraction of your financial capital to the same factors

---

4. Yao and Zhang, "Optimal Life-Cycle Asset Allocation with Housing as Collateral." See also Kraft and Munk, "Optimal Housing, Consumption and Investment Decisions over the Life Cycle."

by allocating a significant portion of your balance sheet assets to a house. In fact, evidence from the U.S.-based Panel Study of Income Dynamics[5] suggests that controlling for levels of wealth, homeowners actually own less stock-based investments, compared to renters, possibly because of this same reason. Stocks are diversified, tradable, and liquid. Houses are not.

Housing over Time: A Human Capital Approach

In sum, a strong argument can be made—absent all the psychic factors involved in the decision—that renting is the optimal choice when you are young.

However, when you are older (say 50 or 60) and you have unlocked a large portion of your illiquid and nontradable human capital and converted it into financial capital, you can afford to "freeze" some financial capital and lock into a home purchase. At that stage, not only do you have more wealth in total, but also your balance sheet (and especially your human capital) is likely not as sensitive to the state of the economy and its disruptive impact on wages. So, Mr. Spock buys his first house—after 25 years of renting—at the age of 50. (Says Spock, *"Nowhere am I so desperately needed as among a shipload of illogical humans."*)

Now, you might justifiably worry here that if you (or Mr. Spock) don't buy a house when you're young, you might never be able to afford a house when you're older. I have heard many real estate agents say that it's important to get a foothold into the real estate market, or you will never be able to afford a house.

Well, I trust that the experience of the last few years has taken some of the air out of this argument. If you examine the inflation-adjusted growth in the price of an average house during the last ten years, as measured by the S&P/Case-Shiller Home Price Index, it equaled only 3.5 percent. And this doesn't adjust for the often enormous cost of maintenance that is never captured in the long-term datasets.

---

5. The PSID is a longitudinal panel survey of U.S. families that measures economic, social, and health factors over the life course and across generations. Data have been collected from the same families and their descendants since 1968.

There's one more dimension that impacts the housing decision and that is the increasing mobility of the labor force. This dimension results in a much higher probability that you might need to relocate for a job, career, or employment opportunities. This is yet another factor that increases the incentive to rent for as long as possible. There is nothing more disruptive to a smooth consumption path (and the practice of Long Division) as having an illiquid and unsellable house serve as an anchor to a region in economic distress.

Finally, if by renting a house (or condo or apartment) instead of buying as soon as possible, you are truly concerned you might miss out on the market, the authors of one of the articles I cited earlier suggest that you hedge and protect yourself against this risk by invest-ing some money in a mutual fund that is linked to real estate prices, such as a real estate investment trust, or REIT.[6] This way, you can participate in the increased value of housing, without having to mow a single lawn or unclog even one drain.

If you would like to calculate the impact of rent-versus-buy deci-sion in your own life, I have created a calculator that can help you work through some scenarios, so you can see what decision makes the most sense in your case and what the impacts are with different vari-ables. Go to www.qwema.ca to do your own analysis.

The Missing Factor: Housing and Social Capital

During most of this chapter (and this book), I have focused my efforts on teasing out the impact of human capital considerations as they apply to financial capital decisions, using basic rules of arith-metic. And yet, although I have emphasized these two forms of capi-tal, I have so far overlooked a third form of capital, which completes the trinity: *social capital*.

Social capital—more so than human capital or financial capital—is not visible to the naked eye, is not easy to measure, and, unlike every other form of capital I've discussed to date, does not belong on the per-sonal balance sheet. Social capital is loosely defined as the collection of networks, cooperation, relationship, norms, mutual aid, faith, and various

---

6. Yao and Zhang, "Optimal Consumption and Portfolio Choices with Risky Hous-ing and Borrowing Constraints."

other forms of "glue" that hold a community together. But what does social capital have to do with housing? There is actually a strong link between home ownership and social capital, which is one of the reasons policy makers in the United States (and, to a lesser extent, in the rest of the world) have encouraged and promoted homeownership.

Please note that I am not veering from my mandate of discussing money milestones and personal finance when I mention the role of social capital. The reality is that social capital also serves a smoothing function. How so? If you live in a community or society with high social capital values, you are much less likely to experience disruptions in your standard of living. Think about the neighborhood or community where you live. If you happen to run out of flour while baking a cake or need to jump-start your vehicle to get to work one morning, how many neighbors within short walking distance would you feel comfortable borrowing the cup of flour or jumper cables from? All of them? Some of them? None of them? And do you know the names of all your immediate neighbors?

These might sound like unimportant and even off-topic questions, but they can have a profound impact on financial matters. Although it doesn't belong on the personal balance sheet, social capital is an asset class you can invest in by creating it. Individuals can do this on a community-specific basis; for example, you can arrange a monthly "neighbors' barbeque" for everyone on the block. Specific communities (and religions and schools) can produce social capital as well. Researchers—mostly sociologists—have developed indices of social capital that they've used to indentify regions of the country that score highly, versus poorly, in this dimension. (Apparently Vermont and Minnesota score highly but Georgia and Tennessee do not.)

At this point, you may be asking, what does all this have to do with housing?

Well, according to a recent study by researchers at the Federal Reserve Bank of Chicago and the Office of the Comptroller of the Currency; housing, social capital, and financial well-being are all intertwined.[7] According to the authors, greater homeownership rates

---

7. Agarwal, Chomsisengphet, and Liu, "Consumer Bankruptcy and Default."

increase the social capital of a neighborhood simply because home-owners (versus renters) face larger transaction costs in selling their house and moving away. This reduced mobility incentivizes home-owners to invest in things that increase their property value, which, in turn, also creates more social capital. So social capital is created as a result of home ownership, and property values rise in the process as well. Although you might not think about the investment you are making when you lend that gallon of milk, the logic of investing in social capital is clear.

Investing in Social Capital

This relationship between social capital and financial well-being then manifests itself in a number of interesting ways. For example, the authors in the previously-noted study obtained detailed records of more than 170,000 individual credit card histories over a two-year period to observe individual payment behavior and bankruptcy filing status for each of these 170,000 individuals. The dataset contained enough information so that the individual's age, address, marital status, and homeownership status could be linked to their credit card behavior and in particular could determine whether they filed for bankruptcy protection during the two-year period.

Now, as you might expect, borrowers living in counties and regions with high unemployment and poor economic conditions and those individuals who have lower income and wealth status experienced higher default rates. No surprise there.

However, what is interesting is the following conclusion. I quote from their study: "An individual who continues to live in his state of birth is 9 percent less likely to default on his credit card and 13 percent less likely to file for bankruptcy, while an individual who moves 190 miles from his state of birth is 17 percent more likely to default and 15 percent more likely to declare bankruptcy." This, of course, is consistent with a social capital story under which the closer you live to your place of birth, the more likely you are to have vested social capital to protect. Along the same lines, it seems that married individuals are 24 percent less likely to default on credit cards and 32 percent less likely to file for bankruptcy. Finally, homeowners—and keep in mind that home ownership provides another proxy for social capital—are 17 percent less likely to default and 25 percent less likely to declare bankruptcy.

In sum, I suspect that people grossly underestimate their home ownership expenditures. They overestimate the amount by which the house will appreciate over time. They tend to live where they work (obviously), which means that their housing capital (which is a subset of financial capital) is exposed to the same economic risks as their human capital. And yet, the one thing an investment in housing might achieve is that it creates its own investment in social capital. Perhaps this one factor outweighs the many other negatives and makes this particular money milestone worth pursuing.

Summary: The Four Principles in Action

- Americans (as well as Canadians) have ADDED significantly to their personal balance sheet allocation to housing over the last few decades. Housing can ADD to your net worth over time. However, even a small decrease in the value of housing can also SUBTRACT value from your personal balance sheet, and the effects of this subtraction can be MULTIPLIED if your household is over-allocated to housing.

- A more rational way to approach your need for shelter is to DIVIDE your spending on a primary residence, if you are a homeowner, into an allocation for shelter (meeting your consumption needs for shelter) and an allocation for investment. Another rational approach that has been advocated by a number of financial economists is to hold off on purchasing a house until you have converted a significant amount of your human capital into financial capital.

- If the cost of the house, today, exceeds the value of your human capital, in all likelihood you shouldn't be a homeowner, period, regardless of how low the (current) monthly payments are or how low the interest rate is. This is likely another one of the most important concepts within strategic financial planning for individuals.

- The role of housing is also connected to another form of capital: social capital. The effects of investing in social capital can MULTIPLY your investment in your home, increasing your financial well-being—and that of your community—in surprising and unexpected ways. So, it's not only about the money after all!

7

Insurance Salesmen and Warranty Peddlers: Are They Smooth Enough?

A few months ago, I went to my local electronics store to get a new cordless telephone because the one in my office had broken after a few years of daily use. After scanning the aisles, I chose a basic unit that cost about $110 and headed to the cash register to pay. Upon handing the salesperson the phone I wanted, she asked, in a bored monotone, a question she'd probably already posed a hundred times so far that day: *Want to buy an extended warranty on that?*

I'm sure you've had the same experience, too, every time you've bought something from any electronics store. Her pitch continued: The warranty would "protect me" for the next two years, and if anything should happen to the phone, I could just return for a new one. She finished her spiel with the announcement that the cost of the warranty was a mere $45 plus tax, payable now.

I was flabbergasted, but she wasn't—she recited the whole thing without displaying any recognition of the irony that protecting the phone would cost *more than 40 percent of the purchase price.* When I asked her if she recommended warranty extension because she *expected* the phone to break in the next two years, her response was "No, but you should still consider the extended warranty"—because I could then "get the same phone" if anything happened to the one I was buying. I then asked whether I could just bring the phone back if it failed and get a new one without buying the extended warranty, and she said that obviously "something" had to be wrong with it to get a free replacement—but that the store's return desk doesn't tend to ask many questions. We sparred back and forth for a couple of rounds that ended when I politely but firmly declined the insurance coverage.

This is not the only silly insurance anecdote I have accumulated over the years, and I am sure you have your own stories of warranties that cost half as much (or more) as the (relatively inexpensive) item they protect. These stories get even more ludicrous, and frustrating, if you actually buy the policy and try to exercise your warranty and make a claim, which is denied or the warranty is invalidated for whatever reason.

But my favorite ridiculous insurance story comes from a phone call I received at home during dinner a few years ago, one night near the end of December. In Toronto, where I live, there's a lovely lake, Lake Ontario, where many people sail their boats in the summer and store them during the winter at various marinas spread across the harbor. That evening, the man on the other end of the phone line claimed to be from the largest property and casualty insurance company in Canada, and he was offering me a special time-limited deal on boat insurance. Apparently the cost of this insurance was going to be increasing by more than one-third at the start of January because the re-insurance treaty (which serves as the protection for the insurance company) was about to expire. He told me that if I transferred my policy to the company he worked for within the next 72 hours, I would save more than $500 on a typical policy. I presume I was erroneously on some database because I told the caller that I don't own a boat and hence had no interest in buying (or transferring) a boat insurance policy. However, that didn't slow him down. He responded that I should still seriously consider the offer because the renewal rates would definitely be increasing in January and that I should act quickly—what did this cold-caller want me to do, go out and buy a boat just so that I could get a good deal on the insurance? (Perhaps I'd call it...*Have I Got a Deal for You!*)

I enjoy telling this boat insurance story to my students because I think it perfectly illustrates a number of myths and misperceptions about the whole field of insurance—in particular, about the kinds of potential losses to insure and the proper role of insurance in our lives. I also think it neatly demonstrates how insurance is largely *sold to* people, rather than *purchased by* them after careful, and rational, evaluation of the alternatives. However, insurance decisions are among the most important money milestones you will encounter in life. This chapter explores how to understand insurance, including insights from the world of human capital thinking.

Insurance from Babylonia to Today

The history of insurance stretches back as far as the second and third millennia BC, when Chinese and Babylonian traders practiced early methods of transferring and distributing risk. The ancient Code of Hammurabi (circa 1790 BC) even included a basic form of insurance, by stipulating that debtors who encountered personal catastrophe (such as flooding, disability, or death) could be relieved of their debts.

The inhabitants of Rhodes invented the concept of the "general average" as a form of property insurance. (And this is the only legal maxim that survives of the great body of law of the Island of Rhodes, known as the *Lex Rhodia*, circa 800 BC.) Merchants whose goods were shipped together would pay a proportionally divided premium, which would be used to reimburse any merchant whose goods were lost during storms or sinkage.[1] The monarchs of ancient Persia were probably the first to introduce the concept of insuring human life, circa 550 BC to 330 BC. At the start of each new year, people would present gifts to the king. The amounts paid were registered by the monarch and, if the gifts were sufficiently large, their value could be repaid up to two times over to the giver in times of trouble. Later, the Greeks and Romans circa 600 AD organized guilds called "benevolent societies" that cared for the families and paid funeral expenses of members upon death.

By 1654, French mathematicians Blaise Pascal and Pierre de Fermat discovered a way to express probabilities and, thereby, understand levels of risk. Pascal's work led to the first actuary tables that were used to calculate insurance rates. These tables formalized the practice of underwriting.

Then, in 1666, the Great Fire of London destroyed around 14,000 buildings. London was still recovering from the plague that ravaged it a year earlier, and many survivors were now homeless. As a response to the chaos and outrage from the Great Fire, groups of underwriters who until that point had dealt exclusively in marine

---

1. Interestingly, this is actually the source of our modern word "average"—it comes from the Arabic *awariya* ("damaged merchandise").

insurance formed companies to offer fire insurance. By 1693, Pascal's work was used to create the first mortality table and what we know today as life insurance soon followed.

Insurance companies flourished in Europe, especially after the Industrial Revolution. But in America, the situation was different: The colonists' lives were rife with risks no insurance company wanted to share. Ultimately, it took another hundred years for insurance to become established in America. The sale of life insurance in the U.S. began in the late 1760s, when the Presbyterian churches in Philadelphia and New York created the Corporation for Relief of the Poor and Distressed Widows and Children of Presbyterian Ministers. Episcopalian priests organized a similar fund in 1769, heralding the start of the life insurance industry in the United States. (I'll touch on just a wee bit more U.S. insurance history in a moment.)

Insurance Purchases: Another Form of Smoothing

But first: recall the "25-to-25" thought experiment I posed to my undergraduate students in Chapter 2 ("What Is the Point of Saving Money Forever?"). However, this time, imagine that instead of being sure to receive some large sum in the distant future, the experiment is framed in terms of losses. Imagine there is a 0.1 percent chance that at some point in your life you will suffer a loss (or have to pay) $1,000,000 because of some natural disaster or unforeseen accident. If this one-in-one-thousand event occurs, you will face a sudden and dramatic reduction in your standard of living. You might have to take on extra debt, accept a second job, or perhaps even file for credit and bankruptcy protection. Moreover, if you've diligently been practicing Long Division, your smoothing apparatus will be destroyed.

Now, what if I offered you an insurance policy that could protect you against this disruption? In exchange for an annual premium of $1,000, you could rest assured that if this catastrophe occurred, the loss would be covered. Would you take this policy? I would. Although my overall standard of living would be reduced marginally because of the extra $1,000 I would be paying every year, this reduction is much less painful to me than the enormous disruption from a sudden million-dollar drop in my net worth would be. (This hypothetical insurance example differs materially from the cordless phone "protection policy" because although the disruption to my standard of living represented by the payment of the extended warranty for the phone is even more trivial, the loss I would experience if that particular phone stopped working is so small it doesn't even register.)

Thus, at its core, insurance is a smoothing mechanism. However, unlike Long Division, insurance doesn't smooth *consumption across time*; instead, it's about smoothing across *different alternative universes*, ones in which you or I experience an unfortunate roll of nature's dice. In one future alternate universe, you don't get hit with the million-dollar catastrophe, and your life turns out just fine. In another, less probable, future alternative universe, you went bankrupt at the age of 40 because you were hit by the million-dollar disaster. (And you didn't insure against this risk.) So, to smooth consumption over all the alternative universes you will encounter across your life cycle, you purchase insurance to protect, or smooth, your lifestyle across all these potential outcomes.

Now, I don't believe that most people actually think this way about insurance. (If they did, no one would offer extended warranties on inexpensive consumer items, or for that matter on boats I don't own.) However, this is my recommended way of viewing the money milestone purchase of insurance.

But this "insurance to smooth" thesis doesn't imply that you should go out and insure every single possible bump or blip in any possible universe. Small losses, such as the failure of a $110 phone after two years of use, should not be insured, unless you are living in extreme poverty on $2 per day like almost half of the world population. (In that case, why are you buying a phone that costs nearly two months' wages?) The $110 loss will not cause a material disruption or unraveling of your family's smooth life-cycle plans. So, I say forget the extended warranty, do not insure against this loss, and don't waste your money on the premiums.

On the other hand, if the event you are insuring against could cause an enormous disruption to your standard of living, go ahead and insure. So, ultimately, you have to consider two aspects of every potential catastrophe. First, what is the *probability* this event will take place (very small, average, or very high), and second, if the catastrophe occurs, what is the *magnitude of the disruption* (very large, substantial, small, miniscule) to your smooth standard of living? My proposition is that you should insure only events that have a potentially disruptive impact on your lifestyle, and only if they have a relatively low probability of occurring. I'll explain more about this two-dimensional approach in a later section. For now remember the following rule for insurance coverage: Buy it for events that are both *catastrophic and unlikely.*

Life Insurance as a Hedge for Your Human Capital: When Young

According to the American Council of Life Insurers, the total amount of life insurance coverage in force today in the United States is approximately $20 trillion dollars.[2] This staggering sum of money would be paid out only if all the insured individuals died at the same time. Short of a widespread fatal epidemic or a gigantic meteorite hitting our planet, the insurance industry can safely assume that this amount will not be paid out all at once. In fact, some of this money might never be paid out at all if people stop paying their premiums and their policies lapse.

If all the insured individuals in the United States died at the same time, that would clearly be a disastrous event for the life insurance industry. But in your own life circumstances, all it takes is one death—your own—to register as a catastrophe. Recall that when you are young, your greatest asset is your untapped (or unmonetized) human capital. Therefore if you die young and with dependents, you've lost—or more to the point, your family and dependants have lost—that future income.

So the proper way to think about life insurance (and disability insurance, critical illness insurance, and even unemployment insurance) is as a *hedge for your human capital.* In the world of finance, a hedge is an investment to limit loss. If something happens to you, the

---

2. At the end of 2007, according to the Canadian Life and Health Insurance Association, 20 million Canadians owned a combined amount of more than $3.1 trillion of life insurance.

insurance company will pay out the death benefit (or face value) of the policy to your beneficiaries.

I explored the concept of insurance as a human capital hedge in my earlier book (*Are You a Stock or a Bond?*). At this point I want to simply emphasize and remind you that as you age and progress through the human life cycle, the argument (and the need) for life insurance to protect human capital is much weaker because the value of human capital declines with age. When you are retired, for example, it is hard to justify the payment of large insurance premiums to protect human capital that has a low value. So, in preparation for retirement, you should have converted a large portion of your human capital into financial capital, and you should thus be more concerned about protecting this financial capital that must now sustain you for the rest of your natural life than protecting your human capital (or your phone!). Indeed, likely the only argument for maintaining a large and permanent insurance policy at advanced ages is for estate planning or tax purposes. Life insurance is about smoothing income for your family and loved ones across alternative future universes: It is not meant as a consolation prize for the living or as a reward to your spouse for putting up with an old cranky nuisance (that would be you, in retirement). If you have insurance at later stages in life, the premiums you've been paying and will continue to pay for many years to come would have likely been better off deposited in some bank account.

According to historians, the origin of the idea that life insurance is for protecting the value of human capital, and that you should accordingly use an estimate of total future earning power to determine a suitable amount of life insurance, is Professor Solomon Huebner. Just shy of a hundred years ago, Huebner taught the first formal courses on life insurance at the Wharton School of Business at the University of Pennsylvania. He also wrote the foundational textbooks on life insurance and helped create the modern insurance industry association.[3] Huebner outlined his "human life value" approach to life insurance in a series of lectures beginning in 1919. An academic review of

---

3. For an interesting history on this impact of Dr. Huebner on the entire insurance industry, see the article by Creek, "Solomon Huebner and the Development of Life Insurance Sales Professionalism."

his impact on the life insurance industry notes, "Huebner encouraged salesmen to calculate a man's career earning potential as his human life value, wrapping the matter of setting an indemnity in the solemn science of economics. He especially urged solicitors to target 'all persons working on a salary, be they ordinary or expert' for life value appeals, for in the professions 'the life value constitutes practically all their business worth.'" So, when economists at the University of Chicago, such as Professor Gary Becker and Professor Theodore Schultz, were talking (in the 1960s and '70s) about the importance of investing in and returns from human capital, they were building on the foundation created (in the 1920s and beyond) by Professor Huebner, who preached the importance of protecting the human capital you already have.

Life Annuities as a Hedge for Your Financial Capital: When Old

Although I discuss the topic of pension and retirement income planning in Chapter 9 ("Retirement: When Is It Time to Shutter the Well and Close the Mine?"), this is a good time to remind you that insurance isn't just about protecting the family against bad things (like death and disability or unemployment); it can also be used to protect the family against something *good*, namely that you live too long! Yes, I know this might sound odd, but nowadays you can actually purchase an insurance policy that will pay out if you live an unexpectedly long time. This is called *longevity insurance*, and it is actively marketed under various generic names by a number of insurance companies in the United States and Canada.

Here's how this works: Think about your future self at the fine old age of 80. You are in good health, relatively active, but retired from regular work many years ago. According to your doctor (who you visit regularly), there's no reason why you won't make it to the age of 95 and even beyond. Today the odds are that a healthy 80-year-old female has a 50/50 chance of living to age 89 (and age 87 for a healthy 80-year-old man). In fact, there is a 25 percent chance that an 80-year-old female will make it to the age of 93 (or 91 for a man). Moreover, the better your health, the greater your expected longevity.

There's even an 11 percent chance for a female, and an 8 percent chance for a male, of seeing 100 and triple digits on the birthday cake.[4] In the United States today there are close to 100,000 people above the age of 100. You might be one of them, either now or later.

Now think about the alternative universe analogy. In 90 out of 100 possible future universes, you do not live to 100 and hence don't have to worry about providing for yourself at that advanced age. However, in 10 out of those 100 possible future universes you do. Will you have enough money saved? Or will you have to reduce your standard of living? Again you are faced with a *smoothing dilemma*. But unlike our 25-to-25 example, this disruption does not come from a sudden accident or calamity that costs millions of dollars: Instead it is a slow and prolonged slide that erodes the purchasing power of your money over time and thus reduces your ability to maintain a smooth and dignified standard of living. So, as I've said, it is possible to purchase insurance so that if you win this particular jackpot, you get either a large up-front or small periodic payment to help meet your expenses. (More on smoothing mechanisms for longevity in Chapter 9.)

However, surprisingly enough, your chances of dying might also be affected not only by your physical health, but also by the health of the economy you're living in. There is some interesting research that seems to indicate that mortality rates (which tell us the rate at which people die at any given age, or the probability of you personally dying during the next year) actually decline in bad economic times. Counter-intuitively, in times when unemployment is above average and the markets are in a funk, fewer people die, which means that people live longer. In contrast, when financial times are good, apparently mortality rates increase. Whether this is because people have more time to exercise and eat carefully in recessions or whether it is due to reduced smoking or even reduced traffic accidents is all subject to speculation in a paper published in the *American Economic Review*.[5] From my perspective though, this phenomenon is more than

---

4. Calculations based on the RP-2000 Healthy Annuitant and the 1996 Annuity 2000 mortality tables, from the Society of Actuaries. See www.soa.org for more.

5. Miller, Page, Stevens, and Filipski, "Why Are Recessions Good for Your Health?"

just a public policy curiosity. For those concerned about the holistic management of risk for the household and the value of all assets on the personal balance sheet, this evidence brings yet another dimension to the interaction between human capital, financial capital, and the role of insurance. If you follow the findings of the research paper, you can almost think of *health itself* as a personal asset class that is negatively correlated to the economic environment and the performance of your stock portfolio. (That is, your health moves in the opposite direction to the economy.) At the extreme, it seems long periods of unemployment and reduced income, paradoxically, might imply that you need to save even more money for retirement. How ironic is that?

What and When Do People Actually Insure?

Like some of the other decisions I have so far addressed, evidence shows how people *actually* make their insurance milestone decisions differs quite substantially from how they *should* make those decisions. For example, the research consensus is that low-income households generally do not have enough life insurance to protect the family if a death of the breadwinner occurs. An article published in the *Journal of Financial Intermediation* reported that a quarter to one-third of American wives are inadequately insured, meaning they would suffer a material loss in their standard of living should their spouses die.[6] These families either do not have life insurance or have too little. In contrast to this underinsurance problem among low-income earners, it appears that high-income households tend to *over-insure* the life of the major breadwinner. In other words, a large number of these people might actually be worth more dead than alive! Economists have a politically correct phrase for this: They call it *a mismatch between insurance holdings and insurance vulnerabilities*. What you see is that while on average people in general might have enough life insurance, this average masks a wide disparity in vulnerabilities across the

---

6. See Auerbach and Kotlikoff, "The Adequacy of Life Insurance Purchases," and Bernheim, Lorni, Gokhale, and Kotlikoff, "The Mismatch Between Life Insurance Holdings and Financial Vulnerabilities."

socioeconomic spectrum. (Again, you can see that averages can conceal as much as they reveal.)

Another puzzling phenomenon regarding the purchase of life insurance was reported by researchers at Florida State University. While examining comprehensive sales data from national insurance companies, the researchers noticed odd and unpredictable spikes in the regional purchase of life insurance. They couldn't explain these results by looking at promotional offers, discounts, or any other supply-driven explanations. But, they noticed that, for example, suddenly and seemingly without cause, weekly sales of life insurance in the State of Georgia would triple. Or over the course of a month, five times as many people would apply for life insurance compared to typical sales volumes.

After scratching their collective heads about this, and running a variety of statistical tests on the numbers, the researchers decided to scan the local papers for clues. Perhaps, they figured, a local celebrity had died, or there had been a major traffic accident fatality or other corresponding sudden increases in mortality. But it turns out, oddly enough, that the answer was not in the *obituaries* section of the newspaper but in the front page and the *weather* sections. The regions with these inexplicable jumps in life insurance purchases had also recently experienced spikes in serious hurricanes and tornados. Now, these natural disasters didn't necessarily kill or even seriously injure anyone. Sure, the *property* damage was extensive, which you'd think might increase the demand for an interest in property and home insurance, but surprisingly, it also increased the demand for life insurance. According to the researchers this irrational effect can actually persist for years after large and well-publicized natural catastrophes. In their words: "Research indicates that the occurrence of a catastrophe may lead to an increase in risk perception, risk mitigation, and insurance purchasing behavior."[7] I think this example actually gets to the core of how most people treat life and other insurance transactions. That is: Our decisions tend to be emotional and fear-driven, as opposed to fully rational. Few consumers treat the insurance milestone as part of the life cycle smoothing exercise I previously

---

7. Fier and Carson, "Catastrophes and the Demand for Life Insurance."

described; however, Table 7.1 provides some illustrations of how to work through insurance purchases rationally.

TABLE 7.1   You Are 45 Years Old. What Are Multiple Paths of the Future?

Event (Possible State of Nature)	Probability It Will Happen to You	Magnitude (If It Happens to You)
Live to 95	11.4%	Unless you are a multimillionaire, with oodles of cash to spare, *get a pension.*
Die within the next five years	0.62%	If you have a family that depends on your income, *get life insurance.*
Lose your toe in an industrial accident	Less than 0.012%	If you work at a job where you need all ten toes, *insure them!*
Asteroid Apophis hits the Earth in 2036	0.0022%	Could wipe out a country the size of France or Germany and kill millions of people. If you're in the strike zone, perhaps move?
Earth gets sucked into a black hole	No reliable data available	We are all dead. Don't bother worrying about it!
Get struck by lightning	5–20%	Can be surprisingly benign, although death from cardiac arrest is common. Get life insurance if you need it, not "lightning-strike insurance."
Get sick from the flu this year	20%	Annoying. A few days of missed work. *Do not insure.*
Your $110 phone breaks	100%	Trivial. No disruption. *No insurance!*

As you can see, some events are extremely likely and not very costly; whereas others are extremely *unlikely* and extremely costly. You want to insure (that is, smooth across alternative universes) only those events that have a relatively small chance of happening and that are likely to disrupt your and your family's standard of living.

I've provided you with some irrational and rational ways to think about insurance milestone decisions. Now you might be wondering how I personally handle these decisions. How rational am I in practice?

Here's my guiding principle; it's the phrase I used earlier: *catastrophic and unlikely.*

Create Your Own Insurance Company: The "Small Risk Fund"

As you gathered from the earlier part of this chapter I (religiously) avoid paying for insurance on any trivial risks that will not overly disrupt my smooth lifestyle. I don't buy extended warranties, trip cancellation insurance, or extra coverage on car rental policies. This saves me quite a bit of money. At the same time, I have also asked my own insurance company to increase my deductibles to the maximum allowed, which means that I personally am liable for the first $1,000 (or so) of damage to my car and the first $5,000 (or so) of damage to my house in the event or a storm, flood, or fire. In addition, although I spent quite a bit of time carefully studying the issue, I also decided not to buy critical illness insurance, which is rather popular in Canada. These gambits save me quite a bit of money on an annual basis. But none of this is irresponsible or neglectful behavior on my part because I have *self-insured*, consistent with the smoothing process I advocate.

You see, I actually keep careful track of all the premiums and fees I have *not* paid. This money represents, after all, a rough estimate of all the damages and costs an insurance company might have to pay me, on average. So, instead of spending the money I've saved on something else, or just ignoring the savings, I deposit those funds in a dedicated account that I call my Personal Insurance Reserve Fund. I manage this account like an insurance company (is supposed to) manages their reserve: risk-free investments only and *no dipping into the cookie jar* (except to cover a loss).

So the account sits (earning a bit of interest) and is tapped into on the unpredictable occasion that our household experiences an unexpected financial battering—something that might have been covered by insurance, had my wife and I decided to buy it. In that case, we tap into the Reserve Fund to cover the replacement cost. Now, let me make this clear: I'm not talking about a rainy day fund or slush account to cover a new roof or resurfacing the driveway. I'm talking about a true insurance reserve fund. Our family constitution (Okay, the one I maintain in my head) stipulates that the fund can be tapped only for expenditures that would have been covered by insurance we declined, and I am careful to deposit all the (hypothetical) premiums into this account. Not surprisingly, I have been forced to tap into this reserve fund over the last few years—for a basement leak and an accidental fender bender that the insurance adjuster gleefully informed me was less than the deductible—but the Reserve Fund is still showing a large surplus and has never been exhausted by any abnormally large claims. (It isn't surprising that I've had to dip into the Reserve Fund because the risks I've decided to self-insure are both relatively common and relatively cheap.) And after all, I still have insurance coverage for the large catastrophic disruptions to my smooth lifestyle. I've created a calculator that enables you to compare risks you should share with an insurer and those you might want to self-insure, plus some estimate of the costs you might save by self-insuring. Go to www.qwema.ca to check it out.

Now, why do I play this game with myself? Why not just merge this fund into our family's general account and manage all the money together?

Behavioral Economics in Practice

Indeed, my behavior demonstrates a number of quirks that behavioral economists such as Richard Thaler have identified and explored. When I ponder my reasons for establishing and maintaining my Insurance Reserve Fund, what I say to myself is usually some variant of: I do this because I want to avoid the regret associated with tapping into the family's general finances if something breaks. (Behavioral economists would call this *mental accounting*, the process by which people group their assets into individual, nonfungible accounts.) I also want to ensure we don't spend the saved money on trivial things (thereby displaying my *loss aversion,* or the strong human preference for avoiding losses as opposed to acquiring gains) and impose discipline in our finances (by using a *commitment device,* which locks me into a course of action I wouldn't ordinarily follow but that produces a desired result). I'm also *anchoring* (or relying heavily on one piece of information when making decisions—identifying "saved money" from my foregone premiums, as opposed to viewing this money neutrally). In this way, I guess I'm a walking example of the realities of behavioral economics; that is, how people actually behave as opposed to how purely rational creatures (what Thaler calls "Econs") would behave.

Now, once again, this might seem like the ultimate behavioral fallacy, creating a mental account to which I attribute losses, but like I've said, my account is more than just psychological (or mental!). If you can't self-insure because you can't keep your sticky fingers off the Insurance Reserve Fund (instead of using it to cover losses, just like an insurance company would), go ahead and buy all the insurance and warranty policies you want. (And I know a boat insurance salesperson you should really talk to.) It's probably cheaper than paying for financial therapy from a behavioral psychologist. However, if you can handle the risk and the disruptions, which will vary in magnitude for different people of different means, go ahead and save the (unpaid) premiums like I do.

My personal Reserve Fund today contains thousands of dollars, which is the sum of all the discounts I received from abnormally high deductibles on my insurance policies. The difference between covering the first $500 of damage (the standard deductible on home insurance) and the first $5,000 in damage can be up to half of the usual premium. The home insurance agent was actually quite reluctant to allow me to do this and made me sign repeatedly that I understood that the company would likely not cover the vast majority of the claims they usually receive. But that was exactly the point: By saving them from paying me a claim 90 percent of the time and covering only the catastrophic losses, I was saving them money for two reasons: one obvious and one subtle. The subtle one is that I, as a homeowner, was signaling to the insurance company that I would take much better care of the property (by having sufficient working smoke detectors and keeping my doors locked). Knowing that I was thus a lower overall financial risk to them, they reduced my premiums even further. Try this yourself. But remember, make sure to save the difference!

Of course, here is the best part of this exercise. If a loss occurs, you don't have to argue with an insurance company, you won't have to dicker with the adjuster or the agent about whether your claim is covered, or worry about whether the policy fine print covers what you actually thought it covered. After all, you are making a claim on your own reserve fund. You only have yourself to argue with.

In closing: The point of insurance is to smooth your lifestyle over alternative universes. Insurance isn't an investment or a form of protective magic. It is important to understand that the investment return from buying insurance is always negative. That is, you can't make money "on average," and the insurance company make money "on average" at the same time. Instead, they charge you—and everyone else—more than the amount they expect to pay out. Otherwise the company would go bankrupt, and you wouldn't get paid either. So, take advantage of this risk pooling mechanism—but don't go there for a leisurely swim.

Summary: The Four Principles in Practice

- There are many decisions and money milestones in life that have an insurance aspect to them, but they tend to be misunderstood. At its core, the purchase of any type of insurance is best understood as a smoothing mechanism.

- However, unlike Long DIVISION that smoothes over your total resources over time, insurance smoothes consumption not over time, but over MULTIPLE possible universes.

- In considering insurance purchases, you need to evaluate both the probability of loss (that is, SUBTRACTION of assets) and the magnitude of the disruption to your standard of living if a loss occurs. A rational approach is to insure only catastrophically unlikely events.

- The real-life world of insurance is full of mismatches and irrationalities. Insurance decisions tend to be emotional and fear-driven. An alternate approach to wasting money on minor warranties and insurance policies is to rationally DIVIDE financial risks into those you will share with an insurer and those you will self-insure. Set up your own Insurance Reserve Fund with the money you save by ADDING and saving the unpaid premiums.

8

Portfolio Construction: What Asset Class Do You Belong To?

Sally Sapher, age 60, is the epitome of financial caution. Despite the thousands of TV commercials, radio announcements, and newspaper stories touting the importance of global stock market investing for financial success, she is steadfast in her avoidance of stock market risk. Her parents lived through the Great Depression, and her uncle is said to have lost a large part of the family fortune in the stock market crash in the late 1920s. So, when Sally resolved to start saving for her retirement, she chose the safest product she could think of: U.S. government Treasury bills. For the past 19 years, at the end of every month, she has deposited $1,000 in her retirement savings account. By the start of 2009 her retirement nest egg had crept up, ever so slowly, to a total of **$326,094**.

In contrast, Sally's next-door neighbor and good friend Robert Rischi is your typical stock junkie. He, like Sally, is 60 years old and he has also been investing $1,000 per month for retirement for the last 19 years. However, unlike Sally, he surrendered to the siren call of the mutual fund and investment industry and has been allocating all his savings to a broad array of U.S. equity funds. In the language of Financial Planning 101, Robert has been *dollar-cost averaging* into the stock market, investing a fixed dollar amount every month. (This means he buys more units when prices are low and fewer when prices are high, as the fund unit prices vary, but the amount he invests monthly does not.)

Robert has been careful to stay away from high-cost mutual funds and concentrated bets on particular industries. After all, he says to himself, his retirement nest egg isn't meant for gambling. Instead, he has carefully calculated his investment time horizon (the period of time he expects to grow his portfolio before needing the money) and his risk tolerance (his ability to handle declines in the value of his portfolio) and implemented the strategy he thinks is bound to pay off. Given what he knows about stock market investing, he thinks his low-cost, diversified approach is a relatively safe way to ensure his nest egg will grow much faster than Sally's.

In the language of economists, Robert has a high degree of investor confidence (in the stock market). To be sure, he's endured some sleep-less nights and restless days over the last few years, and especially over the last 18 months; but he has been adamant in his belief that over the long run the extra market volatility and financial stress he has endured, compared to his neighbor, will pay off with handsome returns. Again in the language of financial economists, Robert is *riding the equity premium* or attempting to take advantage of the difference between a stock market return and a Treasury yield. (The Treasury yield is also known as the "risk-free rate.") In fact, he periodically teases his neighbor Sally about her overly cautious approach to saving for retirement and has promised to invite her to the paradise retirement home in the Caribbean he plans to buy with the wealth he is accumulating.

So where is Robert after his 19 years of investing? Well, at the start of 2009, his portfolio was worth **$319,126**. Yes, you read that correctly: For all the risk Sally shunned, the equity premium she apparently missed, and the ribbing she endured, *she is actually $7,000 ahead of Robert after 19 years.*

Now, wait a minute, you might cry: what exactly was Robert holding all these years? You must be cherry-picking those funds or that period to get those returns! Well, I assumed Robert was holding typical funds linked to U.S. equity indices. I also assumed he was paying expenses of (only) 100 basis points each year. If Robert had been paying 200 basis points in annual fees (which is more typical), his nest egg would be worth only **$282,340**, which is **$43,754 less** than Sally.

And, if you believe that the start of 2009 isn't a fair ending point, consider that it could be much worse. At the start of April 2009, Robert's (hypothetical) portfolio was worth **$286,185**, which is **$43,090 less** than Sally (with expenses at 100 basis points—or **$252,878** at 200 basis points, which is **$66,248 less** than Sally).

Table 8.1 shows Sally and Robert's account values at different points in their investing histories. Take a look for yourself and see how their account values vary over time. I've plotted out their investing results as if they started in January 1993, 1994, and 1995; and as if they stopped in October and December 2008 and March 2009. You can see from the table that Sally's outcomes surpass Robert's in each scenario. Robert has the best outcome if he starts in January 1993 and ends in October 2008; whereas Sally has the best outcome if she starts at the same time as Robert (in January 1993) and ends in March 2009. You can also see that, throughout the chart, Sally's various account values are much closer than Robert's. The range between the top and bottom values for Sally is $47,679, whereas for Robert it is $81,616.

TABLE 8.1   Sally and Robert's Investing Results

Ending Account Value: Sally / Robert	End Date		
	October 2008	December 2008	March 2009
January 1993	226,444 / 253,405	214,013 / 255,451	192,893 / 258,591
January 1994	196,943 / 231,794	186,385 / 233,837	168,371 / 236,965
January 1995	168,618 / 210,912	159,859 / 212,951	144,828 / 216,067

(Start Date rows on left axis: January 1993, January 1994, January 1995. In each cell the upper value is Sally's and the lower circled value is Robert's.)

What Went Wrong?

Writing this in mid-2009, it's impossible to predict how Sally and Robert's situation will look in 2010 or 2011. It could get better for Robert, and worse for Sally. But, as it stood in mid-2009, after almost 15 years of waiting, risk still hasn't paid off for Robert.

Now, even though Sally and Robert aren't real people, Robert's story is, unfortunately, not necessarily uncommon. Perhaps you know a Robert or two. For Robert, and others like him, it seems as though the "stocks for the long run," buy-and-hold approach has not worked out. Indeed, the stocks for the long run mantra is increasingly in question: At the end of June 2009, U.S. stocks have underperformed long-term Treasury bonds for the past 5, 10, 15, 20, and 25 years. In addition, new research on the earliest period of stock returns has suggested there are methodological flaws in how returns have been calculated that should cause investors to seriously question whether what we've been told about stock market returns over the long period holds any water today.[1] Now, I am quite sure that most prudent financial advisors would never advise Robert to allocate 100 percent of his retirement account to equities, whether U.S. or international. Perhaps his portfolio would be tempered with some asset allocation to bonds and other asset classes. The possible allocations are endless—and indeed, some alternate Roberts might be ahead of Sally. At the same time, many others who have been buying and selling (as opposed to simply buying and holding) for the last 20 years have ended with *much worse account values* than all the previously mentioned scenarios. A March 2009 study finds that although the SP500 produced an annualized return of 8.35 percent over the 20-year period ending on December 31, 2008, the average equity investor who jumps in and out of the market had a return of just 1.87 percent during the same period, or less than inflation.[2] Like Robert, the average investor failed to beat even the risk-free return available from T-bills. And consider that beating Sally's results isn't setting the bar very high, given the little skill that implementing her strategy requires.

So what are the alternatives to ending up in Robert's shoes? Surely Sally's strategy isn't the only appropriate investment approach to save for retirement; might Robert's strategy ultimately outperform Sally's? Absolutely. However, the reality is you don't know whether it will, it will take time to find out, and you don't even know how long it might take. Right now, what I do know is that over the 19-year time horizon I examined, which is as long as many people's entire investment savings time span, Robert's strategy did not end up producing a

1. See Zweig, "Does Stock Market Data Really Go Back 200 Years?"
2. DALBAR, Inc., *QAIB 2009*.

premium over Sally's very basic, risk-free approach. And it isn't very useful (to Robert) to suggest that Robert, who wants to retire now, adjust his timeframe to some uncertain period so that his stocks for the long run, buy-and-hold approach has a chance of producing results that surpass Sally's.

So what are investors to do? In the next section, I take a look at some alternative ways to approach investing for retirement, including some new ways to think about your approaches to risk and your labor market income, and—to revisit the Introduction: "Human Capital: Your Greatest Asset"—how to include your human capital when you allocate your overall retirement savings portfolio. These new ways of thinking take us beyond the standard retirement planning concepts of investment time horizons, risk aversion, and investor confidence.

Are You a Stock or a Bond or Something in Between?

I actually wrote an entire book devoted to this topic, so I don't want to repeat myself here or belabor points I've already made. Instead, the purpose of this section is to provide you with an explanation of my thinking about the conditions under which individuals should—and should not—expose their financial capital to stock market risk. I'll also provide you with a method to allocate your investment portfolio in a way that considers your human capital.

At the outset, I'm going to ask you to think differently about your labor and wage income (that is, the money you make at your job) than you probably do now. Our starting point is to think about your labor and wage income like an *investment* with its own investment characteristics. In particular, you're going to examine two dimensions of the investment characteristics of your labor and wage income: namely, their *flexibility* and their *sensitivity to general economic conditions*.

The first dimension that you're going to look at is fairly intuitive: your labor income flexibility. Here's how you can assess this: Consider how much flexibility you have to work overtime in your current job. Can you work for a few extra hours per week or month, if need be, and get paid more? If yes, although your job responsibilities might be limited to 35 hours of work per week, you might also have the ability to expand your supply of labor income—that is, by working longer hours—and thus to convert more of your human capital into financial capital. In this case, your labor market income is flexible. Other dimensions of labor market flexibility include taking an extra job and delaying your expected retirement age.

The flexibility of labor market income varies across occupations and work settings. A nine-to-five employee who works at a large company or as a public servant, for example, might not have any ability to get paid more for working more hours. If you are a schoolteacher, you are paid a fixed salary no matter how many extra hours you put in grading student assignments, following up with parents, or chaperoning school dances. But other workers, like hourly laborers, dentists, and lawyers typically have much more flexibility to work more and thus earn more. The business model for most lawyers in the United States and Canada is the billable hours model, in which law firms bill by the hour (usually in six-minute increments!), and each lawyer carefully tracks and usually attempts to maximize her total billable hours. Similarly, plumbers and construction workers can work far more than "regular" working hours if the jobs are available and the price is right.

The flexibility dimension is an important variable to assessing the investment characteristics of your labor and wage income. If you work in a flexible environment, you have the ability to earn extra greater dividends—whether they are large or small—from your human capital. Conversely, if you work in an environment with little or no flexibility (which we will call a *rigid* environment), there is effectively a cap on the returns you can earn from your human capital.

A second, equally important dimension of the investment characteristics of your labor market income, albeit one that is slightly harder to measure (as it becomes evident only over time), is *the relationship between economic conditions and your compensation*. What this dimension measures is the sensitivity of your career, job, and income to the economic cycle in general and the financial market in particular. Some jobs and careers (and hence some sources of labor market income) are highly correlated to economic cycles, whereas others are not. A public servant (or tenured professor), to give two examples, will receive relatively the same compensation in different economic conditions—that is, whether the SP500 index is up or down, or whether global stock markets are in a bull or bear mode. But there are many other careers whose wage profiles are relatively sensitive to these kinds of changes. Income from careers that are not correlated to economic cycles can be thought of as *bond-like*, whereas income from careers that are correlated can be thought of as *stock-like*.

Now, at the outset of this section, I said I was going to explain my thinking about the conditions under which individuals should and should not expose their financial capital to stock market risk. What I am going to suggest is that *the amount of risk you take with your financial capital should be determined holistically*, by including both human and financial capital in the equation, and by assessing and including the investment characteristics of your income from human capital.

Ok, that's a mouthful. Let's unpack this a bit. The two dimensions I asked you to think about earlier are whether your labor market income is *flexible* (versus *rigid*), and whether it is correlated with financial market cycles (whether it is *stock-like* or *bond-like*). When these two dimensions come together, you can refer to them as FeBo (flexible, bond-like) and RiSo (rigid, stock-like).

All else being equal, having a FeBo-like job—think of a barber who can set his own hours, work on weekends if he wants, and earn income that is relatively immune to a recession—means you can afford to invest a substantial portion of your financial capital in more risky ventures like the stock market. This is because if things don't work out for your financial portfolio, you know that your human capital will not be affected. More important, you can "undo" the damage done to your wealth by a falling stock market by working some extra hours (weekends, late nights) to repair your portfolio. Sure, this isn't your preferred strategy, but it's a backup plan.

In contrast to the barber, think of the investment banker's administrative staff at a large investment house. I consider this to be RiSo human capital. They probably don't have the flexibility to work overtime, and yet if something happens to their company or the stock markets, they are less likely to be employed, less likely to earn a bonus, and less likely to derive dividends from their human capital. They might earn more than the barber, but the RiSo-like characteristics of the job implies that their retirement savings and investments should be allocated more toward safer bonds.

Individuals with rigid (nonflexible) income that is sensitive to the stock market should have little if any equity exposure in their financial capital, regardless of how young and risk-tolerant they are. Why? Again, because they are already exposed to significant risk through the investment characteristics of their labor market income. But those with stable (bond-like) wages that are actually quite flexible, that is, those who can work overtime or weekends, can afford to take risk and should be encouraged—although obviously not required—to do so.

Based on your personal situation, how much of your financial capital should be exposed to stock market risk? To get the answer, I propose a four-step process:

- First, start by creating your total financial balance sheet, listing the value of your existing human capital and the estimated value of your human capital. (If you need a refresher or want help calculating the value of your human capital, flip back to the Introduction. You'll also find an online calculator at www.qwema.ca.)
- Second, DIVIDE your human capital value into a portion that is flexible and bond-like (FeBo); versus rigid and stock-like (RiSo). These are the two extremes of "very safe" and "very risky" human capital. Keep in mind that this will be a rough estimate!
- Next, decide how much overall risk you are comfortable with on your total personal balance sheet and what proportion of risk-free assets you want on your total balance sheet. How many multiple future outcomes are you willing to tolerate? This might lead to, for example, 60 percent in total risky assets and 40 percent in total risk-free assets. Now you have to SUBTRACT the allocations you already have within your human capital.
- Finally, figure out how to allocate the financial capital you have to invest so that the *total* ratio, across your financial and human capital amounts, is the *desired* risky/risk-free ratio previously mentioned.

How Does Your Allocation Measure Up?

Here are some examples that will hopefully make this clearer.

In the first example, you have Giovanni. He is a young salesperson, in his mid-20s, with an estimated $500,000 in human capital. He has also managed to save $100,000 in financial capital. Giovanni works in an industry that is strongly correlated to broader market cycles: He is a salesperson for a pipeline equipment company. Part of his compensation is salary ($45,000), and part is commission (which can add up to another $45,000 in a good year). His salary is guaranteed (that is, bond-like) while his commissions fluctuate with his sales success, which is connected to the broader economy and the demand for pipeline equipment. He has determined that 50 percent of his future expected income is risk-free (bond-like) and 50 percent is risky (stock-like).

Giovanni has also determined his overall risk tolerance. He is comfortable with an overall allocation of 60 percent to risky assets, and 40 percent to risk-free assets. Now the question is: how should he invest his $100,000 of liquid capital to achieve the desired 60/40 split across his holistic portfolio?

Our next example is Bridget. She is a schoolteacher who has just retired. She has an estimated $200,000 in remaining human capital. She thinks that fully 75 percent of the future income from her human capital is bond-like because she will receive a guaranteed pension of about $36,000 per year, and this income is not correlated with the broader economy. (Bridget is now drawing on the implicit human capital she built up as a pensioned worker during her years of employment.) Bridget has allocated 25 percent of her future labor market income to the stock-like category because she provides some after-school tutoring on a part-time basis, and she finds that the amount parents are willing to spend on tutoring varies with the economic cycle. Bridget also has $200,000 in financial capital to invest. Her overall risk tolerance is the same as Giovanni's—because her pension is guaranteed, she feels she can take some risk in her overall portfolio allocation. How should Bridget invest her $200,000 of liquid capital to achieve her desired 60/40 split across her holistic portfolio?

Table 8.2 shows the human and financial capital balances for Giovanni and Bridget, their desired overall portfolio allocation, and the financial capital allocation that correctly allocates their financial capital to attain the desired holistic portfolio allocation.

When you look at our table, you can see that the allocation for your financial capital is *not* the same as your overall portfolio allocation. In fact, when you include your human capital, the allocation of your financial capital might be quite different from your overall target ratio. But this isn't the incorrect allocation; rather, it is correct based on your holistic assets, *human capital included.*

TABLE 8.2   Human and Financial Capital: Invested Together

	Giovanni		Bridget	
Human Capital	Risky	Safe	Risky	Safe
	$250	$250	$50	$150
Total Human Capital	$500		$200	
Financial Capital	+ $100		+ $200	
Total Capital	= $600		= $400	
Desired Holistic Risky/Safe Mix	60%	40%	60%	40%
Implied Holistic Portfolio	$360	$240	$240	$160
Financial Capital Allocation	$110	($10)	$190	$10
	110%	-10%	95%	5%

Note: All dollar values are in thousands

Bridget's case provides a good example—because so much of her expected income from her human capital is bond-like, her financial capital allocation can be weighted very heavily toward risky assets. Our table shows a financial capital allocation for Bridget of 95 percent risky/5 percent risk-free assets. You will notice in the table that Giovanni must invest $110K into the risky (stocks) category in order to maintain a holistic $360K (which is 60% of $600K) in the risky asset. However, he only has $100K at his disposal to invest. So, to achieve his desired allocation he must borrow (or leverage) the other $10K. This results in a financial asset allocation of 110% risky assets and -10% safe assets. In other words, he borrows 10% of the risky portfolio value and invests that as well. In sum, his holistic allocation will be 60% risky and 40% safe. There are many possible permutations, but hopefully you get the point.

Avoiding Robert's Outcome

Was Robert—the individual I started the chapter with, who allocated all his investment nest egg to stocks—wrong? Well, it really depends on what he does for a living. If he is a stock broker or trader, his aggressive equity allocation was inconsistent with his human capital. If he were a barber, perhaps he did the right thing. He probably will have to work some extra time to make up the stock market losses, but his human capital hedged his risky financial capital allocation. Once again, you can't judge the success of the outcome based on their age or risk tolerance alone. The same thing goes for Sally. Did she do the right thing? Well, in hindsight it looks like she did. But, once again, her very safe financial capital allocation would make more sense if her job is more risky and tied (implicitly) to stock market fortunes.

One logical outcome of this type of thinking is that, particularly for an investor whose human capital is "safe" and considerably weighted to producing flexible, bond-like income, the allocation of financial capital (alone) to bonds should *increase* over time as the total balance sheet assets are composed progressively more of financial capital (not human capital).

That is, if you have stable, bond-like labor market income, as you convert your human capital to financial capital, you will want to ensure your overall allocation keeps the correct proportion of risk-free assets. This will keep your total holistic portfolio allocation in balance. In fact, if you do not do this, but maintain the conventional approach to considering your financial capital in isolation from your total personal balance sheet, you run the risk—literally—of being exposed to too much financial risk. You don't want to end up like Robert: faced with a depleted human capital balance and what is, in retrospect, a too-aggressive allocation of your financial capital. Indeed, the approach I've outlined provides a strong underlying rationale for the standard recommendation for investors to move increasingly to fixed income allocations as they age: It isn't because their "risk aversion" has decreased, but that their existing assets have moved from the human capital side of the ledger to the financial capital side, and the correct risky/risk-free allocation should be maintained for the entire personal balance sheet.

If, on the other hand, your labor market income is rigid and stock-like (RiSo), in the early years of your savings you will also want to allocate a higher proportion of your financial capital to safe risk-free assets such as bonds. As you age, and your total balance sheet is (ideally) composed increasingly of financial capital, the proportion of risk you can take with your financial capital will increase while your holistic risky/risk-free ratio will remain constant.

In other words, age or time alone doesn't necessarily determine how much of your nest egg (investment, financial capital) should be allocated to risky stocks versus safe bonds. It really depends on the overall composition of your balance sheet.

It must be noted that there are many other variables in retirement income planning this model doesn't include. We haven't considered tax (see Chapter 5, "Government Tax Authorities: Partners, Adversaries, or Bazaar Merchants?"), pensions (Chapter 9, "Retirement: When Is It Time to Shutter the Well and Close the Mine?"), how to convert financial capital to income streams in retirement, and a whole host of important issues. However, what this chapter intends to provide is a new and hopefully useful way to approach the allocation of your personal financial resources—one which explicitly takes your human capital into account.

Do you now wonder what the proper allocation of your financial assets is, given your holistic personal balance sheet? I have included a calculator that can enable you to work this out for yourself, at www. qwema.ca. You can model different proportions and scenarios to see the varying ideal allocations of your financial capital.

Human Capital Impacts Financial Capital Well Before Your First Job

What you've seen so far is that your total portfolio includes both your human capital and your financial capital. I've recommended that you allocate your financial capital in a way that takes into account the investment characteristics of your human capital. But when is the right time to start thinking about the investment characteristics of your labor market income?

Evidence suggests you should start addressing the interaction between your chosen career (which will affect the value of your human capital and produce your labor market income) and the structure of your portfolio (your financial capital) well before you get your first paying job. A business school professor who studied the career and earnings paths of MBA students graduating during bull (good) and bear (bad) markets wrote a particularly interesting article that illustrates this quite clearly. The study was published in the *Journal of Finance* in late 2008 (which was not a particularly good time to be in the stock market!) and was based on data from a survey of about 2,500 Stanford University MBA students who graduated over the 20-year period from 1976 to 1995.[3] A few results from the study were fairly obvious. For example, if the stock market performed relatively well during the typical two-year period over which students study for an MBA degree, a much greater proportion of graduating students went to work on Wall Street as investment bankers. This is not surprising because it is much more likely that investment banks recruit more MBA grads in good times than bad times. According to the study, in a year in which the SP500 index increased by 20 percent over the long-term average, the probability of entering the investment banking business increased by two percentage points.

Of course, those students who didn't get jobs working for investment banks were not unemployed. They went to work in other, perhaps lower-paying fields, such as consulting or in high tech. And they could always switch jobs later in their career, if they really wanted to work as investment bankers.

However, the rather novel finding from the study is that the initial labor market conditions had a disproportionate impact on future career paths and labor earnings. In other words, the presence of a bull or bear market over the 24 months of the MBA program not only had an impact on their first job, or early wages, but it also had an impact on a student's career as much as 20 years later, through

---

3. Oyer, "The Making of an Investment Banker."

multiple bear and bull markets. That is, it seems as though the conditions that prevailed during MBA students' courses of study (and which affected their chances of working on Wall Street) actually impacted their career paths not just immediately out of school but two decades later! If you went to work on Wall Street right after graduating, your likelihood of working there later on was actually 50 percent higher.

Although it might not be surprising that careers and job paths are rather "sticky," it is interesting to quantify the magnitude of this effect. The study found that 15 years after graduation, investment bankers from Stanford's MBA program could expect to earn $1.2 million per year, whereas management consultants earned half of that, at approximately $645,000 per year. Whether any of these (historical average) numbers will persist going forward remains to be seen. But one thing is certain, the state of the economy and the market can have an enormous impact on your lifetime earnings—not just when you enter the labor market but throughout your career. The final sentence in the article makes this point—and is the reason I have mentioned this study. The author writes, and I quote, "The results also suggest that risk-averse MBA students, especially those interested in Wall Street careers, may want to take actions to insure themselves against the random wealth effects imposed by stock returns while they study. These students should short the stock market upon entering school so that their portfolios hedge their expected labor income."

In finance, short selling—also known as shorting—is the practice of selling assets, usually securities, borrowed from a third party with the intention of buying identical assets back at a later date to return to the lender. A short seller hopes to profit from a decline in the value of the assets, when he will pay less to repurchase the assets than he received on selling them. So in this case, MBA students could use short-selling strategies so that if markets decline while they are in school, thus decreasing their expected salaries upon graduation, they can nevertheless generate personal profits. In essence, this strategy allows the student to profit in both bull and bear markets—in a bull market, from their MBA degree, and in a bear market, from the short selling strategy. In sum: Your current financial capital allocation should be based on the risk classification of your human capital, even before you get your first job!

Can You Take Diversification Smoothing Too Far?

Although I have repeatedly advocated applying the basic laws of arithmetic when it comes to financial planning, and specifically the concept of Long Division smoothing when dealing with spending and investing decisions, there is evidence some people have taken this concept a bit too far when allocating their financial capital to stocks. In other words, they smooth and divide when they really shouldn't. Here is an interesting case in point.

Professor Richard Thaler, from the University of Chicago, along with one of his colleagues, obtained a large dataset of 401(k) plans in the United States.[4] They observed both the number and type of investment funds available for those plans, and how people allocated their savings to different funds, for a large number of employers and plans. They were interested in measuring which mutual funds and menu choices were more popular and whether certain funds received greater allocations than others. This is like asking the manager of a large restaurant which items on the buffet are more popular (pie) and which are of lesser interest (salad).

Oddly enough, the researchers found that all items on the menu (of mutual funds) were *equally popular*. They all had allocations that were relatively even, regardless of the number of options available. In other words, if Company A had three equity-based mutual funds and two bond-based mutual funds, the typical participant in the plan would split their asset allocation so that 60 percent was in equity funds, and 40 percent was in bond funds, and the money would be evenly distributed and with equal amounts across the five funds. On the other hand, if Company B's 401(k) plan had only a single equity fund and four bond funds, they found most people in that plan would allocate 20 percent of their savings to equity funds and 80 percent to bonds. This is like Company A restaurant offering three different salads and two different types of pie at a buffet, so your meal is made up of three bowls of salad and two pieces of pie. However, at Company

---

4. Benartzi and Thaler, "Naïve Diversification Strategies in Defined Contribution Savings Plans."

B's restaurant, your meal is now one bowl of salad and four slices of pie—as though the menu determined the outcomes![5] Clearly, this is a form of long division and smoothing, but it does not make much sense. After all, just because the owner of the restaurant decided to offer six different kinds of pie at the dessert buffet, doesn't mean you should have one slice of each for lunch.

History of Ideas: Credit, Where It's Due

This idea, that you should determine how to invest your financial capital by including your human capital can, as many other ideas I have discussed in this book, be traced back to well-known financial economists. In particular, a 1992 article I read as a graduate student greatly influenced my thinking in this matter.[6] Using the techniques and idea of Dynamic Control Theory (which I touched on in the Introduction), the authors and well-known scholars—Professors Bodie, Merton, and Samuelson—derived the optimal amount of stocks and bonds that investors should hold over the course of their life cycle, taking into account the investment characteristics of their labor income. It might come as no surprise that the authors, who are all professors with tenure and job security, concluded that, early in life, investors with relatively stable income could afford to take on much more stock market risk.

What About the Rest of Us? Back to Human Capital

So how much risk should you take? What proportion of your assets should be in risk-free securities, and what proportion should be invested in stock markets in search of the equity premium? I've argued in this chapter that your equity allocation should depend much less on your so-called time horizon, your hard-to-measure risk aversion, or your at-times fickle confidence in the stock market, and much more on the *composition* and *structure* of your personal balance sheet. That is: If your job is reasonably secure, your pension is protected, and your income is predictable, go ahead and take some

---

5. This effect was dubbed the *1/n heuristic*, which describes the finding that the greater the number of choices available *(n)*, the finer people sliced their investment allocations.

6. Bodie, Merton, and Samuelson. "Labor Supply Flexibility and Portfolio Choice in a Life-Cycle Model."

stock market risk with the nonessential funds. Thus, I personally am still very heavily allocated to equities because I have a secure job with a defined benefit pension. At the same time, it should be clear from the example of Sally and Robert that there's nothing wrong with being risk-averse, particularly if your time horizon is finite (and whose isn't?)—it might even be the winning strategy.

Here's the bottom line: The long run can be very long indeed. The financial planning theories you have used to quantify the "probability of regret" or the shortfall risk from equity investing must be revised after the new statistical evidence uncovered during the past year. To paraphrase one of the greatest economists of our time, Professor and Nobel Laureate Paul Samuelson, *the long-run case for equities should not be oversold.*[7]

Summary: The Four Principles in Practice

- Asset allocation investment decisions should take into account the value and the risk characteristics of your human capital and financial capital, jointly. The proper way to do this is to ADD the value of your human capital to your financial capital to arrive at total capital otherwise known as economic net worth. Then, based on your comfort level and risk tolerance, decide how much of your total economic net worth you want in safe investments and how much you want in risky investments, for example 60 percent risky and 40 percent safe. That is the total asset allocation.

- Then, SUBTRACT from this amount the part of your human capital that you estimate is relatively safe and the amount that

---

7. Perhaps the shortest version of Paul Samuelson's rebuttal of the "stocks for the long run" argument is summarized in this 1997 quote: "Canny risk averters should always keep in mind, in a rational, non-paranoid way, the pains they will feel in...probability-calculated bad-outcome scenarios. (Ask yourself: Will stepping down toward a poverty level, when that rarely but inevitably does happen, outweigh for me the pleasures that occur in those likely outcomes when my equity nest egg does increase?) When we each do that, those of who truly are more risk averse will rationally hedge our bets by limiting our exposure to volatile equities." As quoted in Bodie, "Letter to the Editor: Are Stocks the Best Investment for the Long Run?"

you estimate is relatively risky. Then DIVIDE or allocate the remaining financial capital so that the proper allocation is maintained for your total capital

- This approach is very different from the traditional approach that completely ignores human capital and allocates and partitions only financial capital. If you erroneously adopt the traditional approach, you may well end up with MULTIPLE exposures to investments you already have embedded by virtue of your job. This is yet another one of the most important strategic concepts in financial planning for individuals.

9

Retirement: When Is It Time to Shutter the Well and Close the Mine?

A few years ago, one of my older colleagues at work decided to retire at the age of 65 after a distinguished teaching career. He had been anxiously anticipating this for many years and had even bought a "countdown clock" for his desk as the official date loomed on the horizon. And so, with much fanfare we, his friends and associates, arranged a large retirement party in his honor a few weeks before his scheduled last day at work. As you might expect, he gave a brief but emotional speech detailing his mixed feelings about leaving the place where he had spent more than 25 years of his working life and talked about his plans to move to a warmer climate, take up sailing, and do all the wonderful things he didn't have time for while he was working. Yes, this anecdote sounds a little hackneyed, but with an estimated 1.8 million of baby boomers turning 65 every year starting in 2011,[1] I suspect these kinds of retirement parties and speeches are common in workplaces across North America.

As the final day approached, our retiree even helped us interview and hire his replacement, who promptly moved into his office and took over his teaching obligations. And so, on that last day at the end of June, when we all enviously shook his hand as he made his way to the university parking lot one last time, we wondered if and when he would ever come back to visit.

It was therefore quite a big surprise when a mere six months later he appeared in our faculty lounge with a smile that wasn't quite as

---

1. North Dakota State Economic Brief, vol. 17 (no. 10), October 2008.

wide as it had been just half a year earlier. Apparently, he wanted to teach again! He said he'd had enough of what he called "the longest vacation in my life." He missed the work and wanted the stimulation of teaching (at least part-time). Moreover, the rumors were, I am told, that his investment portfolio had not turned out quite as well as he had expected, he had underestimated the cost of retirement, and hence he missed his former, pre-retirement salary.

Unfortunately, although he had contributed to university life for more than a quarter of a century, there was little we could do in return for him. Our employer's rules (at the time) were clear: After you retired and started receiving your pension, you couldn't turn back the clock. Retirement was thus an irreversible money milestone. We had already given away his office, reallocated his teaching, and found a replacement for his committee work. Sure, we could try to locate a part-time or temporary substitute-teacher position for him on an ad hoc basis, but the old job was gone. Obviously, he had "exercised his option" to retire prematurely. Whether for financial or psychological reasons, he pulled the trigger too soon.

This story demonstrates one of the reasons why I, personally, intensely dislike the word "retirement." In my view, the binary concept of retirement as we understand it now—as a fixed point before which you are working at 100 percent and after which you are not working at all—is increasingly unworkable. It's also meaningless to the millions of people who, unlike my colleague, find themselves out of the work force by chance rather than by choice. I prefer to think of this money milestone not as a switch to be flipped, but as *the point in your financial life cycle when your human capital has expired*, and all you have left on your personal balance sheet is financial capital.

This viewpoint provides us with a new place to stand. That is, if you think of the transition not as "retirement" but as the point at which you begin to draw on financial capital, not human capital, to sustain yourself in life, the true challenge of this milestone becomes apparent. Although early in life the focus of financial planning is nurturing, investing in, and protecting your human capital, when the vast majority of your wealth is in financial capital format, it is critical to start protecting that as well. Up to that point, you've been monetizing your human capital to provide an income stream. After that point, you need to create an income stream without relying on your human capital.

Over the next few pages, I provide some concrete suggestions about how to allocate or invest that critical financial capital—as you approach and anticipate this money milestone—to create a dignified standard of living for the remainder of your life. In particular, I discuss the role of pensions, annuities, and other products that help manage and meet your personal liabilities.

Why Are Pensions So Important?

At its financial core, a classical Defined Benefit pension plan is the *ultimate smoothing machine*. It's institutionalized Long Division on a formulaic autopilot. How so? Most typical Defined Benefit pension formulas work something like this: After many years of work (at the same company), you are entitled to stay home, relax—and still be paid. Now, as you might expect, the "relaxation paycheck" is not as generous as the "work paycheck." It is usually calculated by multiplying the number of years you worked at the company by your final salary around the date you decide to stay home, and then by two percent. So, for example, if you provide labor services to the company for 30 years and you earn $100,000 per year toward the end of your career, the company would then pay you an annual pension of 30 times $100,000 times 2 percent, which is $60,000 per year for the rest of your life! And, if you worked at the company for 35 years, this formula provides that you'd get $70,000 for life. This income would be guaranteed to never decline but might actually increase if the pension plan was generous enough to offer a cost-of-living adjustment to offset inflation. The basic rule for pensions is this: The greater your salary when you stop working and the greater the number of years of service you provided, the greater your pension.

What a great deal (for those who have a Defined Benefit pension). You might live for another 20 or 30 years, perhaps all the way to the age of 100, and still be paid regularly. And, if you have a partner or spouse, many plans will continue the payment to them if you personally are no longer around. (This is known as a survivorship benefit.) Perhaps this is why they call these the "golden years."

Now think about this arrangement within the context of our previous discussions on smoothing consumption and practicing Long Division over your life cycle. Imagine that you work for a company

with a Defined Benefit plan over your entire employable life of 45
years (from the ages of 20 to 65) and then stop working. With 45
years of service multiplied by 2 percent, you would get about 90
percent of your preretirement salary. Considering that you can
probably save on a variety of work-related expenses such as trans-
portation and clothing when you aren't working, the amount of
money you have available to spend might equal, or even surpass,
what it was when you received a paycheck, not a pension. The result
is that you could have saved absolutely nothing during 45 years
(independent of your pension contributions) and still have the
smoothest of consumption profiles. There would be no jagged drops
or *discontinuities* (as the economists call it) in your standard of living. You would be the poster child for Long Division! More important, because it provides you with a lifetime of income—no matter
how long you live—it also insures you against longevity risk, which I
alluded to in Chapter 7 ("Insurance Salesmen and Warranty Peddlers: Are They Smooth Enough?"). And, if other investments (like
money in the stock market, or the value of your house) decline in
value, the pension annuity still pays. So a Defined Benefit pension
smoothes, insures, diversifies, and hedges you all at once. *Sign me
up!*

Now, unexpected inflation, progressive tax brackets, and other
annoying real-world frictions can throw a wrench into simple rules of
arithmetic and the smoothing provided by a Defined Benefit pension
plan, but you get the idea. Basically, a Defined Benefit plan attempts
to put into practice what I consider the fundamental axiom of life-
cycle wealth management—that is, smoothing or Long Division.

Pensions Are a Dying Breed

However, the reality is that today many employers are cutting
back on their Defined Benefit pensions and replacing them with
Defined Contribution arrangements. These, in my opinion, aren't
really pensions at all. Instead, Defined Contribution pensions are
(tax-sheltered) investment accounts where the employee (that's you)
contributes money each month, with some amount of matching contribution from your employer—and then you decide how to invest or
allocate these funds. There are no guarantees provided or benefits

promised when you eventually decide to leave the employer, whether at retirement or before. These are called "defined contribution" plans precisely because the only thing defined is the amount of your own contribution. Typical examples of Defined Contribution savings plans include a 401(k) or 403(b) plan in the United States, or a group RRSP plan in Canada. In theory, Defined Contribution plans were designed to accumulate a sum of money that would generate an income stream equivalent to Defined Benefit pensions. But in light of the horrendous performance of the stock market during 2008 and 2009, and some of the evidence I discussed in Chapter 8 ("Portfolio Construction: What Asset Class Do You Belong To?"), one has to wonder if these Defined Contribution saving accounts will provide sufficient resources for retirees.

Here's what the landscape looks like in mid-2009: If you work in the private sector in the United States, which means that you work for a company and are not a government employee, there is only a 20 percent chance that you are covered by a Defined Benefit plan. Most likely, you are a member of Defined Contribution savings plan at best, a group that includes some 43 percent of private industry workers. In contrast, if you are part of the public sector, either state or federal (think fire fighter, police officer, teacher, judge, and senator), there is a 79 percent chance you are part of Defined Benefit pension plan.[2] Notice the contrast here: Most private sector workers have no pension; most public sector workers do.

In Canada, the numbers are similar: Private sector pension plan participation is at 23 percent, and in the public sector, 80 percent of workers participate in Defined Benefit pensions.[3] However, because the relative and per capita size of the public sector is much larger in Canada than in the United States, the proportion of total workers with Defined Benefit pensions is higher in Canada.[4] What this means

---

2. Statistics in this paragraph are from the Bureau of Labor Statistics' *National Compensation Survey: Employee Benefits in Private Industry*, available at http://www.bls.gov/NCS/.

3. Pierlot, "A Pension in Every Pot."

4. Public sector employment stands at about 6.3 percent of the total U.S. labor force versus 19.7 percent in Canada. U.S. data from Bureau of Labor Statistics, Canadian data from Statistics Canada.

is that in Canada, the shift from Defined Benefit to Defined Contribution pensions is also taking place, but at a much slower rate.[5] The pension coverage numbers have not always looked as lopsided as they do now, and many years ago most large private sector companies actually offered all their employees a Defined Benefit plan. But in the last few decades, and especially the last few years, the trend has reversed. For example, although in the year 2009 the percent of private sector workers who are part of a Defined Benefit plan is 20 percent; in 1974, the percent was almost double at 44 percent.[6] In fact, the number of corporate Defined Benefit pension plans in the U.S. has plummeted by nearly 75 percent since 1985.[7] *Pension plans are dying.*

Why has this happened? I could fill a whole book on this topic (actually, I have, and do not want to repeat myself here),[8] but in short, the pension industry has experienced something of a "perfect storm," and they have weathered it with rather faulty navigational equipment. Pension plan assets have been invested in stocks and other risky instruments that didn't quite earn the returns the sponsors and managers estimated. Also, the liabilities of these plans continued to increase as people increasingly selected early retirement and late deaths (that is, people are living longer), which increased the burden on the plan. Likewise, pension regulation has been faulty in that it allowed some company and most public sector pension plans to hide or at least obscure the true value of their liabilities. But, another important factor—and one that cannot be blamed on poor management—is that many employees over the last few decades, especially the younger ones, saw little value in a benefit that tied them to one company. Many younger workers argued that they wanted mobility and portability, and the chance they would stay at the same company for 30 years was remote. So, they asked employers to switch to savings-type arrangements, especially during the equity bull run of the 1990s when an annual return of 20 percent from the stock market was expected by all.

---

5. Tamagno, *Occupational Pension Plans in Canada.*
6. Employee Benefit Research Institute, "The Decline of Private-Sector Defined Benefit Promises."
7. Pension Benefit Guaranty Corporation, *Pension Insurance Data Book 2007.*
8. See particularly the introduction to *Are You a Stock or a Bond?* called "Pensions are Dying; Long live Pensions."

All these different demographic and labor market trends have left future retirees (including the many baby boomers on the verge of retirement today) with a shrinking pot of money and no guarantees. In the language of the holistic balance sheet, as pensions have moved from Defined Benefit to Defined Contribution and even disappeared, retirement income liabilities have shifted from the *corporate* to the *personal* balance sheet. In this new reality, you might have a more marketable and portable human capital than before, you might have a large sum of financial capital (the Defined Contribution plan) you are managing, but you now also have to face the liabilities.

This trend of declining pension coverage, to me, is truly a shame, given the strong link between true (Defined Benefit) pensions and life cycle smoothing. What you are left with is the increasing personal importance of the "retirement" milestone for today's workforce. That is, providing for your income needs over your lifetime after you have left the paid labor force is increasingly up to you.

Retirees with Pension Annuity Income Are Happier

My pro-pension message is more than just about achieving the economist's goal of smoothing consumption or insuring against longevity risk. One of the consequences of defined contribution and other nonguaranteed forms of retirement income is that the employee (then retiree) needs to make all the investment and allocation decisions on their own, as opposed to receiving guaranteed sums with no investor discretion. Although the capacity to make your own investment decisions—with the inherent capacity to "beat" the implicit return contained on a Defined Benefit pension option—might seem tempting when you are a young employee, you need to keep in mind that you will be responsible for making those investment decisions for the remainder of your life. And as you age, your capacity to and interest in allocating assets and rebalancing retirement accounts might diminish, although your need for effective and appropriate investment management will not.

Behavioral financial research suggests that individuals in retirement who are receiving the bulk of their income from stable, guaranteed, lifetime sources are actually much happier. In addition, as retirees age into their 90s and beyond—when nearly 40 percent of the population is affected by Alzheimer's and other forms of dementia—it becomes critical that people's income be placed on autopilot.[9] One interesting study has attempted to draw connections between the life satisfaction of retirees and the *degree of annuitization* of their sources of income in retirement.[10] The study used data from interviews of households with people ages 51 and older, gathered over a long time period from 1992 to 2000. The total number of people interviewed was approximately 40,800; and many of them have been interviewed every second year since 1992. The participants were asked a detailed series of questions about their expectations and their experience of life in retirement. Then, the researchers matched up the degree of satisfaction expressed by study participants with the extent to which participants were receiving annuitized income (from Social Security and private Defined Benefit pensions). This study finds that "the more people can count on lifelong guaranteed pensions, the more satisfied they are with their retirement." In addition, satisfaction among people with lifelong guaranteed pensions lasts longer than among people without Defined Benefit pensions—in contrast to retirees without Defined Benefit pensions, who tend to experience decreasing rates of satisfaction as they move further into retirement. This was true across all income levels.

The study theorizes that perhaps people without a Defined Benefit pension become increasingly anxious about outliving their savings as they age.

Another study found, interestingly and somewhat shockingly, that your chances of happiness in retirement are highest if you have a Defined Benefit pension, second highest if you have no pension, *and lowest of all if you have only a Defined Contribution pension.* The authors speculate that this surprising result might show the effect of

---

9. Plassman et al, "Prevalence of Dementia in the United States."
10. Panis, "Annuities and Retirement Satisfaction."

the relatively high personal risk run by those with Defined Contribution plans.[11]

Florida's Elderly, Pension Choices, and My Brush with Bush

But what do people actually choose, when presented with a choice between a Defined Benefit pension and something else? Do they choose the ultimate smoothing mechanism? The answer to this question lies in one of the oldest states in the United States (in terms of population), Florida.

During a 12-month period ending in mid-2003, each one of the approximately 625,000 government employees who were members of the Florida pension fund were presented with a unique decision. Each existing and new employee had the option to switch from a traditional *pension plan* to a self-managed *investment plan*. In other words, they could either keep their existing pension plan or take the lump-sum value of their retirement pension—which for some was a number in the hundreds of thousands of dollars—and invest the proceeds themselves in a wide range of carefully-vetted mutual funds consisting of conventional stock and bond choices.

In contrast to many employees facing similar dilemmas in the private sector, some of whom I discuss later, this was an honest choice and not a forced conversion. They didn't have to switch. They could maintain the status quo and remain in their current traditional Defined Benefit pension plan up to and into retirement and beyond. Nevertheless, switching to the investment plan had both plusses and minuses. If your investments did well, you might end up with a much larger sum of money. Alternatively, if your investment choices flopped, you might end up with less. Clearly, the decision was not an easy one to make, and either way it had long-term, significant financial implications. This is why the state was careful in determining which products they allowed into the investment plan and what annuities employees were allowed to select upon retirement. In fact, among the many other precautions taken by the state, they also

---

11. Bender, *The Well-Being of Retirees*.

launched an extensive advertisement and education campaign to explain these options to people in detail. They even hired the Nobel-prize-winning economist William Sharpe from Stanford University to star in a commercial targeted at state employees.

Investment Plans Versus Pension Plans— What Would You Choose?

One of the important things about the experiment in Florida is that the new Defined Contribution plan (technically an optional 401[a] plan) was referenced and labeled in all educational and pro-motional material as an "investment plan," whereas the existing plan was called a "pension plan." This was more than just a "word game" or attempt at semantics: There is an important difference between a true pension plan versus a 401(a), 401(k), 403(b), or any other plan. An investment plan is *not* a pension plan; it is a tax-sheltered invest-ment account. The account will (hopefully) grow over time, the investment returns will (hopefully) beat inflation, and the nest egg will ideally provide a nice cushion for your retirement. However, at some point you need to turn this into an actual income stream that provides you with a respectable income for the rest of your life. In a pension plan, the income stream is provided automatically (allowing you to practice Long Division automatically). In an investment plan— or any similarly labeled account—the responsibility is up to you.

I actually had a rather limited role in all this tumult to help the state administrators decide what type of investment should be allowed in the Defined Contribution plan, and specifically to help select individual annuity choices at retirement for the Defined Contribution plan. Now, these individual annuities are likely one of the most controversial and confusing financial instruments in the financial market place today— and I discuss this more in the conclusion to this chapter—but for now let me just mention that my job was to help explain which, if any, annu-ities made sense for the plan.

So, here is the fundamental question—and it is one that is at the crux of this chapter. Put yourself in a Florida state employee's shoes. Would you take $200,000 now (for example) in lieu of a pension and invest it yourself, together with all the contributions you would receive over the next 10 to 20 years until your retirement? Or would you say "no thanks" to the offer and just wait until retirement and take a Defined Benefit pension based on your 35 years of service, one which would entitle you to a guaranteed $40,000 per year (for example) for the rest of your life? Indeed, some employees had to make this decision with numbers far greater than $200,000. For people with many years of service, higher salaries, or both, the numbers reached into the millions of dollars.

I'm sure many people actually face a similar decision at retirement. What would you do? Do you think you could manage and invest the funds yourself and thus grow the money to an amount that would generate a greater lifetime income compared to a pension? What if you live much longer than you expected? What if the market declines just when you are about to retire? What if inflation is higher than expected? It's a tough choice, no question! And yet, if demographics and corporate trends are any indication, many millions of Americans will be making this exact choice over the next five to ten years: They have a *number* (an amount in an account) and must decide how to convert it into a *pension* (income for life).

Now, you might think that the state was trying to bribe or even worse, outfox their employees. But I can tell you that this was definitely not the case. For those who planned to stay employed by the state of Florida, staying in the *pension plan* was the best choice. However, for those who were uncertain the length of time they would remain, or for those who truly believed they could do a better job managing the money themselves, the *investment plan* made perfect and fair sense. In fact, the state bent over backward to make this a fair choice by giving everybody the option to convert into the investment plan and then "switch back" into the pension plan at some point before retirement. This was no cheap gift. According to some research I conducted and published with a co-author in the *Journal of Risk and Insurance* in 2004, this option was quite valuable.[12] We estimated most Floridians would take the investment plan and then exercise the option to return to a pension, later, prior to retirement.

---

12. Milevsky and Promislow, "Florida: Pension Election from Defined Benefit to Defined Contribution and Back."

And so, to conclude the story, when the dust settled on this massive pension experiment, a mere 4 percent of the people who got the offer decided to convert or transfer from the pension plan to the investment plan. Yes, you read that correctly; only four in a hundred people decided to take the responsibility of accumulating funds and providing an income stream in retirement upon themselves. The majority of Floridians were effectively saying, *I do not want a number, I want a pension*.

Now, Florida wasn't an isolated case of one lone southern state trying to do away with its Defined Benefit pension plan by stealth. Many other states have considered or are in the process of considering the same move, and have followed the results of Florida's process quite closely. Moreover, the U.S. government, which is responsible for Social Security, the largest Defined Benefit plan on the planet, might even go the same route one day. As unlikely as it seems given the recent performance of the stock market, many commentators (many more Republicans than Democrats, not surprisingly) have advocated that the U.S. should follow the model set out in Florida and allow people to opt out of the Defined Benefit aspect of Social Security. In fact, although the proposal was heavily criticized and then abandoned, one of President G.W. Bush's campaign platforms in the 2000 election was to offer Americans individual accounts as an optional alternative to Social Security, similar to Florida's plan. Isn't it interesting that during the same time, the president's younger brother was overseeing the Florida experiment? Boy, I would have loved to be a fly on the wall at their Thanksgiving dinner.

Do Retirees Smoothly Transition into Retirement?

One of the best places in which to observe whether real people prefer smoother consumption over their life cycle, and to see whether they practice what I have called Long Division, occurs at retirement. The few years around the point at which people stop working provide an ideal point at which to measure whether people are smoothing. This is especially the case for individuals who do not have a substantial pension and suddenly (with no more human capital) have to live off their accumulated savings and financial capital. If people are rational and forward-looking when planning their financial affairs, one would not expect to see large drops or gaps in living standards, but a smooth ride. However, if people are not practicing Long Division, they will wake up at retirement and realize they have to tighten their belt.

Unfortunately, though, at first glance the empirical evidence doesn't seem supportive of the rational life cycle smoothing hypothesis. Instead, what is often observed is declining spending in retirement. Economists actually have a name for this: They call it the *retirement-consumption puzzle*, and it has been documented in a variety of countries around the world and over extensive periods of time.[13] Here's the puzzle: People spend much less and seem to live on greatly reduced consumption rates in retirement than they did before retiring. Now, sure, there is obviously a reduction in work-related costs (dry-cleaning your suits, commuting to work), but the evidence suggests reductions of as much as 30 percent compared to pre-retirees who are still working and earning wages from their human capital. Why is the drop so great?

Some researchers at the University of Chicago and the Federal Reserve Bank have provided a solution for this 30 percent drop puzzle, and they could support their explanation using a rather clever dataset of food diaries, as they note in their research published in the *Journal of Political Economy*.[14] According to them, it is important to differentiate between *consumption* and *expenditures*. At first glance, the two might seem to be synonyms for each other, but in fact, consumption is a much broader category. The distinction is more than just semantics. It gets at the heart of one of the main axiomatic suggestions in this book—to practice Long Division.

Here's the explanation. When you spend $50 to buy some ingredients to bake a special cake, your observable expenditures are $50. However, if you spend two hours driving around town looking for these ingredients and then spend another three hours baking the cake itself, your total spending is more than $50. Don't forget the five hours! In fact, if you price your time at $10 per hour, your true

13. Hurd and Rohwedder, "The Retirement-Consumption Puzzle."
14. Hurst and Aguilar, "Consumption vs. Expenditure."

consumption was $50 in cold hard cash and another $50 in the imputed cost of time. Thus, you really spent $100 baking the cake.

What the study found was that although retirees might appear to be spending less than one would expect in the first few years of retirement, they are, in fact, substituting their personal time and spending that time instead! Economists call this "home production." If you focus exclusively on the dollars and cents flowing out of their bank account, you will miss the possibly larger flow of (the dollar value of) time—you won't solve the puzzle.

Now, this is more than just a frivolous accounting exercise: It actually helps refine our understanding of life-cycle planning. This research can serve a warning sign to those who blithely think they will need "much less" when they retire. Maybe you've seen the evidence of retirees with (lower) spending getting by on less. Or you might have personal evidence from a relative who does not spend very much in retirement. Yet, it would be dangerous to extrapolate this anecdotal evidence to your own retirement. In all likelihood your great-aunt is spending more time cooking her own food, shopping for a better deal on milk and eggs, or standing in line for a half hour to get the early bird dinner special at Denny's in Boca. This doesn't imply you will be doing the same during your own retirement. You have to be willing to substitute large amounts of your own time to reduce your expenditures, or cash outflows. But your total consumption (properly defined to include your time) might only be marginally, if at all, lower.

Don't Count on Pennies from Heaven to Smooth Your Retirement Ride

Now, you might be thinking that none of this applies to you, as you personally expect to receive an inheritance to help fund your expenses in retirement. For years, media stories have reported on the coming "biggest wealth transfer in history," as the parents of boomer children leave legacies after death. In fact, a 2006 study showed that some 1.5 million Canadians were counting on an inheritance to fund their retirement, and in a recent survey, fully one-third of Canadian boomers said they expected to receive an inheritance with an average value of $150,600. In addition, 64 percent of those surveyed in 2006 said they had carried debt into retirement, presumably expecting to reduce or eliminate it with an inheritance.

However, as the first wave of boomers inherits funds, reality is falling far below expectations. The average inheritance received by Canadians in 2006 was $56,000; fully $100,000 below the average expected amount. And in the United States, as well, the numbers don't look much different: Recent reports have found that for boomers who had already received an inheritance by 2004, the average value was just $64,000; and that of those Americans who had received inheritances, only 6.9 percent got more than $100,000.[15] The message is clear: Don't expect lump-sum bailouts to smooth your retirement ride.

Is It Better to Get a Lump Sum? The Military View

Despite the considerable psychological evidence that most retirees say they are "happier" when they receive an income from a lifetime annuity (that is, a Defined Benefit pension) compared to those generating their own cash flow from a portfolio of investments (that is, a Defined Contribution pension), there are important exceptions to this rule, especially when people are younger. Some prefer to take their nest egg as a lump sum at retirement and create their own personal pension plan. There are many legitimate reasons for this. For example, one fear that people have—which biases them toward taking a lump sum—is that they might have an (medical) emergency that require large sums of money, quickly. Selecting an annuity would make it hard to react to such emergencies. Another legitimate concern is the fear of default or bankruptcy on the part of the entity paying the pension annuity. There are thousands of airline pilots (who worked for United Airlines) and engineers (who worked for Nortel) and steel workers (employed by Bethlehem Steel) who deeply regret not having taken their lump-sum pension entitlements as soon and as early as possible. One would expect that these are the exceptions to the rule and perhaps extreme cases. But are they? To this end, there

---

15. All figures from BMO Retirement Institute, "Passing It On."

is actually an interesting study that quantified exactly how much more "a bird in the hand" is worth more than "two in the bush."

In January of 1992, the U.S Department of Defense (DoD) began a drawdown program among mid-career military personnel, in an attempt to scale down the size of U.S. defense forces. You can think of this as an early retirement of sorts, which was partially driven by the collapse of the Soviet Union and the reduced need for a large military force. The original 1991 *Defense Authorization Act* directed the DoD to reduce the military by approximately 400,000 by the year 1995, which represented a 25 percent reduction.

Over the same period, approximately 65,000 of those military personnel, who had between 5 and 20 years of service, were offered an interesting financial choice, which is directly related to our discussion of pensions and annuities. According to a study published in the *American Economic Review* in 2001, each one of these 65,000 individuals was asked to choose between receiving a separation benefit in the form of a lump-sum payment or instead taking their entitlement as an annual annuity.[16] In terms of their rank, the group included 11,000 officers and 55,000 enlisted personnel. Guess what the majority decided to do?

Now, the authors in the *American Economic Review* study make clear that the choice was fair and unbiased, similar to the choices offered to participants in the state of Florida's experiment previously described. First, on average, the present value of the promised annuity payments was actually much higher—using market interest rates at the time of approximately 8 percent—compared to the lump-sum payment. In other words, if you took the lump sum and invested this amount at the going long-term government rate of 8 percent, you would NOT be able to generate the annuity payments yourself.

Here is a typical (or idealized) situation to help understand the trade-off. The separating service member was given the choice between $50,000 upfront (today) and a periodic annuity of $800 per month for the next 20 years. If you add up the 20 years times 12 payments per year you get 240 x $800, or $192,000 in total. Now, obviously, this $192,000 was to be received over a very long period, so it is incorrect to simply add up the 240 payments. These must be *discounted* and converted into present value terms. (You may recall

---

16. Warner and Pleeter, "The Personal Discount Rate."

the concept of discounting from Chapter 2, "What Is the Point of Saving Money Forever?")

At the time this offer was given (around 1992), long-term (risk-free) interest rates were approximately 7 percent per year. So, under a 7 percent rate the discounted value was $100,000. This was still double the $50,000 cash offer. Even under a 15 percent discount rate the present value was $60,000. It was only under a 19 percent rate that the discounted value of the $800 per month would equal $50,000. In other words, the individual would have to invest the $50,000 lump sum (if they picked this instead of the annuity) to earn a guaranteed 19 percent per year to generate the same $800 per month for life amount.

This disparity was why the economists within the DoD estimated most people would take the (relatively generous) annuity instead of the (relatively meager) lump sum. After all, the only way the lump sum would generate an ongoing cash flow on the order of magnitude of the annuity payment, was if they could guarantee an investment return of 19 percent per year.

Taking Their Lumps

And yet, as you could tell from the way in which I have been setting up the story so far, the vast majority of military personal did not take the periodic annuity. They took the lump sum. In particular, among the enlisted personnel with less than 10 years of service, more than 90 percent took the lump sum. Among those with less than 10 years of service, over half took the lump sum. Now, you can't argue that "these folks just needed the money" because in theory they could have borrowed against an annuity payment (or perhaps even sold it) if they so chose. As you would also expect, there was a big difference between personnel in the Army, Navy, and Air Force, which are the three branches of the U.S. military. The Air Force officers were the most likely to select the periodic annuity (55 percent of them chose the annuity), whereas a fully 95 percent of enlisted army (nonofficers) selected the lump sum.

All of this is rather puzzling, especially when you remember that most retired people like pension annuities. Why wouldn't the same apply to payments earlier in life (at the age of 40 or 50)? After all, the deck was heavily stacked toward picking the periodic annuity. In fact, this demand for immediacy is observed with lottery winners who are given a choice between a lump sum and periodic annuity.[17] And there are a number of companies who offer to convert your annuity into cash (...at a discount rate of 21 percent).

Ironically, the authors of the study concluded that because so many people selected the lump sum, despite the fact the annuity was worth almost twice as much, these (suboptimal?) choices actually saved the U.S. taxpayers $1.7 billion in severance costs.

Now, some might wonder if this choice was driven by tax considerations, medical concerns, and other such factors. However, the researchers determined that the choices did not affect the benefits (or after-tax payments) received by these individuals. It is also hard to argue that the U.S. government would renege or default on the annuity promise to the U.S. military—after all, they're the ones with the guns! Nor can you pin this decision on a lack of sophistication or lack of education—these are Air Force pilots and officers, after all. These folks can figure out how to land an F16 on a ship in the middle of the ocean. I'm sure they can work out the present value of an annuity and compare it with a lump sum.

So, perhaps the takeaway is what behavioral economists called anchoring.[18] If somebody suddenly and out of the blue offers you a sum of money, or an offer to take it as a periodic annuity, chances are people want the money now and do not take the annuity. (Although I would argue you should take the annuity when the equivalent rate is 19 percent!) They have *anchored* on the lump sum available today, as opposed to a stream of income, in smaller amounts, that will flow at some point later, even if the stream of income adds up to a larger amount than the lump sum, over time. In contrast, when people work for an employer for 10, 20, or 30 years under the *expectation* that they will get a pension one day, and they are given the option of converting this into a defined contribution plan (à la Florida), they would rather have the safety and security of the lifetime pension. That is, they have

---

17. See, for example, comments from Dr. Joel Slemrod (Professor of Economics at the University of Michigan) as quoted in Fox, "The Curious Capitalist: How the Payoff Decisions of Lottery Winners Have Shifted the Income Distribution."

18. Thaler and Sunstein, *Nudge: Improving Decisions about Health, Wealth and Happiness.*

anchored on the pension, not on a lump sum. This is especially true when you consider the vast sums of money lost within 401(k) and IRA plans, in the stock market, over the most recent decade.

Women and Annuities

While on the topic of pension annuities, it seems that although there is a general reluctance to take a lump sum of money and convert it into a life annuity, women are actually more amenable to annuities than men. It is unclear whether this is due to the higher (apparent) risk aversion of women, or whether it appeals to a different aspect of the female psyche, but according to another study published in the *American Economic Review*, when experiment subjects were asked to choose between pension lump sums versus annuities, women choose the annuity option more often.[19] Now, granted, this evidence comes from questionnaires and hypotheticals, as opposed to real, live, choices made by retirees, but the results should still resonate with readers.

The fact that wealthier (female) individuals live longer compared to individuals with lower net worth (and especially males) is well established in the economics and actuarial research literature. For example, according to the study, a 70-year-old male who happens to be in the lowest 20th percentile of the population in terms of wealth (that is, 80 percent of the population are wealthier) can expect to live six more years to the age of 76. In contrast, a 70 year-old female who is at the 80th percentile of the population in terms of wealth (that is, only 20 percent are wealthier) can expect to live 16 more years to the age of 86. The extra 10 years of required income and spending for the wealthier female compared to the poorer male should have an enormous impact on observed financial behavior both before and after retirement. All else being equal, if you think in terms of Long Division and smoothing of consumption over the life cycle, you would expect to see wealthier individuals—which implies a longer life expectancy in retirement—saving proportionally more and spending proportionally less compared to averages and conventional wisdom.

---

19. Agnew, Anderson, Gerlach, and Szykman. "Who Chooses Annuities?"

This finding was actually observed and documented by the researchers when they examined numbers from a dataset called the Dynamics of the Oldest Old (AHEAD).[20] It is more than just some empirical verification of an economic theory; it has practical implications as well. That is, the small but noticeable group of people who seem to be over-saving in their working years ("Why is mom such a tightwad?") or under-spending in their retirement years ("Why is grandma so stingy?") might actually be practicing a more sophisticated form of Long Division over a much longer life.

Final Recommendations: Get a Pension, from Somewhere

After reading the last few pages you might be wondering: geez, what can I do if my employer doesn't offer a defined benefit pension? Am I out of luck, doomed to an unhappy, less-wealthy retirement?

Well, you might try to speak to your local human resources department, or even your boss, to see if they can do something about it. Unfortunately, though, this is not likely to be a fruitful conversation. More practically, I would suggest you look into buying your own defined benefit retirement pension on the open market. This is not as esoteric or difficult as it might sound. Insurance companies have been selling stand-alone pensions for centuries, often under generic names like "guaranteed living income benefits" or "single premium income annuities." Now, this is not the place to delve into the minutia of these instruments, which I discussed in my previous book, *Are You a Stock or a Bond?* Instead, I recommend you seek some professional advice to create a personal pension plan. However, to get you started, I've created a calculator at www.qwema.ca. that enables you to estimate the price for a single premium income annuity, which you could use to create your own pension plan in retirement.

---

20. Assets and Health Dynamics of the Oldest-Old (AHEAD) is a national survey of community-based Americans born in 1923 or earlier. It is sponsored by the National Institute on Aging. The focus of the AHEAD survey is to understand the impacts and interrelationships of changes and transitions for older Americans in three major domains: health, finances, and family.

Finally, where does all of this leave you? Ideally, make sure some of your household retirement income comes from a pension that pays lifetime income for the rest of your life—even if you have to create your own "pension plan" using purchased annuities. This insures you against longevity (something I discussed in Chapter 7) and will likely make you a happier retiree. In addition, most important, if somebody wants to offer you the choice between a relatively low lump sum and a relatively higher periodic annuity, or the choice between a Defined Benefit pension and a Defined Contribution investment account, remember what happened in sunny Florida. Those folks know retirement.

Summary: The Four Principles in Practice

- "Retirement" is best understood not as a sudden switch but as the point in your financial life cycle when your human capital has been largely SUBTRACTED and removed, and what you have left on your personal balance sheet is the financial capital you have ADDED over time. Retirement is when the human capital expires.

- Defined benefit pensions are the "ultimate smoothing mechanism" and can be thought of as an institutionalized version of Long DIVISION. Pensions smooth, insure, diversify, and hedge all at once. There is also evidence that pensions make retired people happier!

- Given the evidence in favor of annuitization (which is just another type of pension), the recommendation is that if you are given a choice, MULTIPLY your chances of success by allocating some of your nest egg to the Defined Benefit pension (while working) or the income annuity (while retired). You might need to create your own annuitized income in retirement to ensure you have a smooth life cycle ride.

Conclusion:
Four Principles to Guide All Financial Decisions and Money Milestones

During the last few years I have been extremely fortunate to meet thousands of ordinary Americans (and Canadians) at book signings and public lectures all over North America. During the receptions and cocktails that are inexorably associated with these events, I have had the opportunity to hear from many individuals about their financial successes, their woes, and travails. I have been asked for personal and detailed financial advice (which I am extremely reluctant to offer), and I have also received my fair share of criticism for things I have said and written in previous books and various media articles. These impromptu discussions with ordinary investors from Vancouver to Miami and from San Diego to Halifax have enabled me to learn a tremendous amount about common financial attitudes and decisions outside of the academic ivory tower.

And, when the opportunity has allowed itself, I have also managed to conduct some informal research that makes all the shrimp cocktails[1] worthwhile. In fact, by now I have asked this question thousands of times, and perhaps you have responded to this as well. I ask:

What was the **worst** financial decision you made in your life?

When asked this question, some people reply immediately, and others take a few minutes and wait to hear what others had to say. Yet,

---

1. Ok. Technically I don't eat shrimp. But I'm sure you get the point.

for the most part, every single person can recall—and quite vividly— some bad financial decision they made in the past. During the frightening period around fall 2008, when banks and insurance companies were on the verge of failing all around us, answers to this question were self-evident: everybody regretted the stocks and mutual funds they held. Then as the real estate crisis played itself out, people regretted the house they purchased. I also heard from people who regretted the business deal they partnered on; they regretted the job they accepted; they regretted the tenant they rented their apartment to; they regretted the car that turned out to be a lemon; and so on. The replies were fast and furious and easy for people to recollect.

To misquote the great Frank Sinatra, in today's economy, we've all had quite a few regrets. Hey, who doesn't have a lousy mutual fund they should have sold months ago, or an expensive house they shouldn't have bought, or a great investment they missed out on. Nearly everyone has some personal or anecdotal story of financial regret, usually employing the general syntax: "If only I had...back when...we would be rich today...." Often these stories are nostalgically transmitted from parents to children and across generations, which can influence financial attitudes towards risk taking and decision making for decades. Everyone has some financial decision they regret.

But then, with these same audiences and groups I follow up with a subsequent question:

What was the **best** financial decision you made in your life?

Oddly enough, the replies to this question are fewer and farther between. The best decision is not immediately obvious or easy to recollect. Yes, I occasionally hear of the apocryphal penny stock that has "done very well" or the special mutual fund that "worked out nicely," but there is much less conviction and feeling compared to the decisions they regret. Sure, a handful of people talk nostalgically about the decision to get married or even the decision to get divorced. One or two mention their grandkids (not the kids, oddly). I even had one person tell me that the best decision was buying a lottery ticket a few years ago, which ended-up winning the jackpot! Yet, one thing is quite clear. The memories aren't as vivid, the stories aren't as clear, and the examples are few. Does this imply that most of their decisions have been failures? I doubt it. I believe they are not thinking broadly enough about what constitutes a regretless financial decision.

Indeed, rarely do people include human capital considerations as part of their financial decisions, despite the fact they have a much greater impact on their personal balance sheet. I never heard people say to me in response to my question: going to college, or not majoring in art, or not taking a particular job after college, or insuring the house that never burned down was the best decision I made.

In fact, these same individuals with so many financial regrets rarely recollect the fuzzy decisions they made years ago with little fanfare, which paved the way for their relative prosperity and thriving daily life. Who commits to memory the job offer they didn't take from the company they don't remember, which then happened to declare bankruptcy a few years later? Or what about the mutual fund they briefly considered purchasing, but then forgot about, that was eventually frozen or liquidated for pennies on the dollar? Think about it. You might remember the rare near-miss, but what about the much more frequent far-miss? Alas, it seems that human beings are hard-wired to unearth some regret from nearly all outcomes.

Making the best decision at each money milestone in your life is just as important as NOT making the wrong one, but is obviously less memorable. As I have argued in this book, it is very important to properly identify all the money milestones in our life and approach them in a more strategic manner. Do this by recognizing the interaction between all disparate factors that impact the assets and liabilities on you personal balance sheet.

Create a Decision-Making Process for All Money Milestones

When I have an opportunity, I ask a third and final follow-up question with these audiences: *What was the process you went through to make the best financial decision?* Alas, here is where I get few, if any, replies. Often there is dead silence. Few people went through a process to help make the decision. I find this to be the most surprising response of all. People remember the outcome and not the process.

According to the Webster dictionary the word *decision* is synonymous with "the act of reaching a conclusion." Notice the emphasis on the word reaching and conclusion. Yet, few people I spoke to could pinpoint or remember these "acts" of reaching conclusions. They all remember the lousy and regrettable outcomes, and some remember the beneficial ones, but few, if any, remember the process itself.

Moreover, it seems that many people I talk to are confusing the decision itself—which might have been flawless—and the outcome that was terrible. (That is, they remember the failure, not the success.)

The behavioral economics literature indicates that people don't seem to make financial decisions; instead—and excuse the colloquial expression—they kind of just fall into them. After the fact, yes, they talk about it being a success or failure. They blame somebody for talking them into the decision, or not thinking about it enough before the decision. But by not having a decision process in place, they were setting themselves up for regret.

The last few years of financial volatility, economic turmoil, and even scholarly research have caused many diligent practitioners and prudent individuals to throw up their arms in despair and pretty much give up on commonsense financial planning. Stock markets have proven to be much less efficient and rational than previously believed. Well-diversified portfolios dropped by more than 50 percent over less than 12 months, and large financial institutions with decades of profitable history collapsed seemingly overnight. Add to these catastrophes the increasing scholarly research that demonstrates how people's brains aren't wired to properly and rationally balance risk and return, and you can't help but succumb to those who simply want to live for the moment. And yet, with all this negative evidence, you still have to make financial decisions. How do you deal with the money milestones in your life? What's the main insight?

According to a famous Jewish story that has been transmitted from parents to children over the generations, approximately two thousand years ago a Talmudic scholar by the name of Hillel was asked by a religious skeptic to summarize the entire body of Jewish knowledge and tradition, "while standing on one foot." This is roughly equivalent to asking for a summary of the Encyclopedia Britannica while riding down an elevator. Hillel responded with what is now a classic Judeo-Christian proverb, "What is hateful to you, do not do unto your neighbor." The rest, he said, was just commentary.

I obviously can't summarize the main idea in this book while standing on one foot (despite the many media requests[2] to do so) nor can I recap 60,000 words in one charmingly witty sentence. However, I would like to conclude by suggesting four unifying and guiding principles to help navigate all of life's money milestones.

PRINCIPLE 1: ADDITION—Identify the true value of all your financial and human capital resources. Your human capital is your most valuable asset for most of your working life. It represents the discounted value of your future wages. This asset tends to be undervalued and underappreciated, especially early in life. As you progress through the human life cycle, you convert (hidden) human capital into (visible) financial capital by saving and investing. Both forms of capital belong on the holistic personal balance sheet and determine your net worth—*you must add your human capital to your financial capital to truly understand your financial position in life*.

PRINCPLE 2: SUBTRACTION—Recognize and budget for all the hidden liabilities in your future. A truly healthy and realistic holistic balance sheet will account for the hidden liabilities on your personal balance sheet. Many of the money milestones you might pass through in life can add to the hidden liabilities side of your personal balance sheet—notably marriage and children, although both might strengthen and add to your assets over time. Your capacity to generate income from your human capital also can create hidden liabilities, in that its loss creates a gap that you need to fill. A clear-eyed view at your life circumstances through the lens of human capital can help you identify, hedge, and bridge all the liabilities you encounter in life. *Don't add assets without subtracting any corresponding liabilities*.

---

2. It should be worth noting that Hillel's contemporary and nemesis Shamai responded to the same request by telling the skeptic to effectively go jump in the lake. I have great sympathy and admiration for Shamai's approach.

PRINCIPLE 3: DIVISION—Plan to spend your total resources evenly and smoothly over time. When you recognize and account for the value of all the assets on your personal balance sheet, devise a long-term consumption (or spending) plan that spreads your total (human and financial) resources over your entire life cycle. It makes little sense to starve yourself for decades so that you can enjoy life in middle age, or when you are old and frail. Likewise, if you "live it up" today without any consideration for tomorrow, you might regret this as well. *Think long term and avoid foreseeable disruptions by budgeting for all predictable liabilities.*

PRINCIPLE 4: MULTIPLICATION—Prepare for many alternative and unexpected universes. Recognize that there are many different future paths of your evolving human life cycle. At each instant in time there are an infinite number of money paths and states of nature over which your future can develop. You owe it to yourself to consider all of them, today. Make sure that you make decisions that help smooth your consumption over all possible paths and not just the expected or hoped-for path. So, insure against all catastrophic and unforeseeable disruptions. *Be a smooth operator over time and space.*

Notice that I deliberately didn't include those tiresome financial sound bites such as "buy low and sell high" or "live within your financial means" or "buy term insurance and invest the difference" or "buy stocks for the long run" or "keep an emergency reserve of three month's salary" or "education pays" or other such nuggets that have actually become titles of entire tomes in personal finance. Despite their popularity, these sound bites don't actually help unify all the money milestones—and they all stem from some underlying principle or viewpoint, but they don't express it.

Therefore, our random tour of Italian women, Florida's lottery winners, Minnesotan taxpayers, African grandmothers, and overweight Japanese borrowers—and the many other characters I introduced you to in this book—should remind you that although some consumers are quite clever about managing their financial affairs, many others are not. But one thing is certain: *Money milestones are universal.*

I think that my four guiding principles should help connect the dots for many dispersed financial decisions in your life. For example, investing in what appears to be costly education actually maximizes the value of your human capital (Chapter 1); whereas borrowing money or living beyond your immediate means and income isn't necessarily inappropriate (Chapters 2 and 3) provided it smoothes the ups and downs. Children might cause an immediate reduction in disposable income and noticeable reduction in your financial capital but might also defuse some long-term retirement liabilities (Chapter 4), in addition to the many other nonfinancial pleasures they can bring. Remember, also, that a fraction of your human capital dividends belongs to your lifetime partner, the tax authority; which is why you must be vigilant to ensure your partner doesn't claim more than a fair share (Chapter 5). Buying a house might seem like the most disruptive of all financial transactions, but in fact it hedges future liabilities (Chapter 6), even though it is not prudent for all. In the same vein, life, property, and other insurance policies help smooth your consumption across alternative universes (Chapter 7), whereas retirement planning (Chapter 9) and investment allocation (Chapter 8) are about practicing long division over time so that you are protected against the surprising risk of a long life.

To quote the parting words of Mr. Spock from the mythical planet of Vulcan—who is likely the only entity who is rational enough to perfectly smooth consumption across time and space—may you live long and prosper.

THE PERFECT JOB FOR ME!

Everyone has the choice of what to be,
I shall pick the one which will be a pleasure to me.
Maybe a fun job and one which makes money,
Or perhaps my boss should be a little bit funny.
The job of a sanitation engineer might be right,
But smelling the awful scent of garbage would not be a delight.
Rotten food, diapers, or an old broken toy,
Picking them up would not be a joy.
Then the profession of a teacher came to my mind,
But all those students screaming and not being so kind,
Calling out answers and yelling out at me,
I think I'll change my mind of what I should be.
Maybe an interior designer would be fun,
Picking out carpets for everyone,
Yellow wall orange wall pink wall too,
I think that's what I'll decide to do.
Occupations galore so many jobs for you and me,
Let's not regret our jobs and pick a fantastic one to be.

—Natalie Abigail Milevsky, Age 10
   Spring 2009, Toronto

References

Agarwal, Sumit, John C. Driscoll, Xavier Gabaix, and David I. Laibson. "The Age of Reason: Financial Decisions Over the Lifecycle." October 21, 2008. Available at SSRN: http://ssrn.com/abstract=973790.

_____, S. Chomsisengphet, and C. Liu. "Consumer Bankruptcy and Default: The Role of Individual Social Capital." May 22, 2009, available at SSRN: http://ssrn.com/abstract=1408757.

Agnew, J.R., L.R. Anderson, J.R. Gerlach, and L.R. Szykman. "Who Chooses Annuities? An Experimental Investigation of the Role of Gender, Framing and Defaults." *American Economic Review*, Papers and Proceedings, 2008. Volume 98 (2): 418-22.

Ando, Albert, and Franco Modigliani. "The 'Life Cycle' Hypothesis of Saving: Aggregate Implications and Tests." *The American Economic Review* 53, no. 1 (March 1963): 55–84.

Auerbach, Alan J., and Laurence J. Kotlikoff. "The Adequacy of Life Insurance Purchases." *Journal of Financial Intermediation* 1, no. 3 (1991): 215–241.

Badenhausen, Kurt. "The Most Lucrative College Majors." *Forbes*, June 18, 2008.

Barber, B.M., and T. Odean. "Boys Will Be Boys: Gender, Overconfidence and Common Stock Investments." *Quarterly Journal of Economics* 116 (2001): 261–289.

Barr, M.S., and J.K. Dokko. *Paying to Save: Tax Withholding and Asset Allocation Among Low and Moderate Income Tax Payers*. Washington, D.C.: Federal Reserve Board, 2007.

Baum, Sandy, and Jennifer Ma. *Trends in College Pricing.* The College Board, 2008. Available at www.collegeboard.com/trends.

———, and Kathleen Payea. *Trends in Student Aid.* The College Board, 2008. Available at www.collegeboard.com/trends.

Bayard, Justin, and Edith-Elizabeth Greenlee. *Graduating in Canada: Profile, Labour Market Outcomes and Student Debt of the Class of 2005.* Statistics Canada, Culture, Tourism and Centre for Education Studies, April 22, 2009.

Beck, Barbara. "A Slow-Burning Fuse: A Special Report on Ageing Populations." *The Economist,* June 27–July 3, 2009.

Becker, G. *Human Capital: A Theoretical and Empirical Analysis with Special Reference to Education* (3rd ed.). Chicago: University of Chicago Press, 1993.

Benartzi, Shlomo, and Richard Thaler, "Naïve Diversification Strategies in Defined Contribution Saving Plans." *American Economic Review* 91, no. 1 (2001): 79–98.

Bender, Keith A. *The Well-Being of Retirees: Evidence Using Subjective Data.* Boston: Center for Retirement Research at Boston College, October 2004.

Bernheim, B. Douglas, Lorenzo Forni, Jagadeesh Gokhale, and Laurence J. Kotlikoff. "The Mismatch between Life Insurance Holdings and Financial Vulnerabilities: Evidence from the Health and Retirement Survey." Federal Reserve Bank of Cleveland Working Paper 0109, 2001.

Bertocchi, Graziella, Marianna Brunetti, and Costanza Torricelli. "Marriage and Other Risky Assets: A Portfolio Approach." IZA Discussion Paper No. 3975, 2009. Available at SSRN: http://ssrn.com/abstract=1336092.

Blumenthal, M., C. Christian, and J. Slemrod. "The Determinants of Income Tax Compliance: Evidence from a Controlled Experiment in Minnesota." NBER Working Paper #6575, May 1998.

BMO Retirement Institute, "Passing It On: What Will Future Inheritances Look Like?" BMO Retirement Institute, July 2009.

Bodie, Zvi, Robert C. Merton, and William F. Samuelson. "Labor Supply Flexibility and Portfolio Choice in a Life-Cycle Model." *Journal of Economic Dynamics and Control* 16, no. 3–4 (1992): 427–449.

_____. "Letter to the Editor: Are Stocks the Best Investment for the Long Run?" *Economist's Voice*. The Berkeley Electronic Press, February 2009.

Brewer, Dominic J., Eric R. Eide, and Ronald G. Ehrenberg. "Does it Pay to Attend an Elite Private College? Cross Cohort Evidence on the Effects of College Quality on Earnings." NBER Working Paper No. 5613, June 1996.

Bucks, Brian K., Arthur B. Kennickell, Traci L. Mach, and Kevin B. Moore. "Changes in U.S. Family Finances from 2004 to 2007: Evidence from the Survey of Consumer Finances." *Federal Reserve Bulletin* 95 (2009): A1–56.

Cigno, Alessandro. "How to Avoid a Pension Crisis: A Question of Intelligent System Design." CESifo Working Paper Series No. 2590, March 2009. Available at SSRN: http://ssrn.com/abstract=1368114.

Cole, Shawn, and Gauri Kartini Shastry. "Smart Money: The Effect of Education, Cognitive Ability, and Financial Literacy on Financial Market Participation." Harvard Business School Working Paper Number 09-071, 2009.

Collins, Daryl, Johnathan Morduch, Stuart Rutherford, and Orlanda Ruthven. *Portfolios of the Poor: How the World's Poor Live on $2 a Day*. Princeton, N.J.: Princeton University Press, 2009.

Creek, Drew Vande. "Solomon Huebner and the Development of Life Insurance Sales Professionalism, 1905–1927," *Enterprise & Society: The International Journal of Business History* 6, no. 4: 646–681.

DALBAR, Inc. *QAIB 2009: Extract of Quantitative Analysis of Investor Behavior*. DALBAR, Inc. Boston, March 2009.

De Nardi, Mariacristina, Eric French, and John Bailey B. Jones. "Life Expectancy and Old Age Savings." FRB of Chicago Working Paper No. 2008-18, January 9, 2009. Available at SSRN: http://ssrn. com/abstract=1311478.

Dickson, J.M., and J.B. Shoven. "Ranking Mutual Funds on an After-Tax Basis." NBER Working Paper #4393, 1993.

Dublin, Louis Israel, and Alfred J. Lotka. *The Money Value of a Man*. New York: Arno Press, 1977.

Duflo, Esther. "Grandmothers and Granddaughters: Old-Age Pensions and Intrahousehold Allocation in South Africa." *World Bank Economic Review* 17, no. 1 (June 2003): 1–25.

Employee Benefit Research Institute, "The Decline of Private-Sector Defined Benefit Promises and Annuity Payments: What Will It Mean?" Employee Benefit Research Institute 25, no. 4 (July 2004).

European Commission, Economic and Financial Affairs Directorate. *The 2009 Ageing Report: Economic and Budgetary Projections from the EU-27 Member States (2008–2060)*. Brussels: European Communities, 2009.

Fier, Stephen G., and James M. Carson. "Catastrophes and the Demand for Life Insurance." (January 27, 2009). Florida State University Working Paper. Available at SSRN: http://ssrn.com/abstract=1333755.

Fox, Justin. "The Curious Capitalist: How the Payoff Decisions of Lottery Winners Have Shifted the Income Distribution." *Time Magazine*, March 6, 2007.

Friedman, Milton. *Capitalism and Freedom*. Chicago: University of Chicago Press, 1962.

_____. "The Role of Government in Education." In *Economics and the Public Interest*, edited by Robert A. Solo. New Brunswick N.J.: Rutgers University Press, 1955.

Goldman, Dana P., and Elizabeth A. McGlynn. "U.S. Health Care: Facts about Cost, Access and Quality." Santa Monica: RAND Corporation, 2005.

Hankins, Scott, Mark Hoekstra, and Paige Marta Skiba. "The Ticket to Easy Street? The Financial Consequences of Winning the Lottery." Vanderbilt Law and Economics Research Paper No. 09-01, April 27, 2009. Available at SSRN: http://ssrn.com/abstract=1324845.

"How Undergraduate Students Use Credit Cards: Sallie Mae's National Study of Usage Rates and Trends 2009." April 2009. Available at http://www.salliemae.com.

Hurd, M., and S. Rohwedder. "The Retirement-Consumption Puzzle: Anticipated and Actual Declines in Spending at Retirement." NBER, Working Paper #9586, March 2003.

Hurst, E., and M. Aguilar. "Consumption vs. Expenditure." *Journal of Political Economy* 113, no. 5 (2005): 919–948.

Ikeda, Shinsuke, Myong-Il Kang, and Fumio Ohtake. "Fat Debtors: Time Discounting, Its Anomalies, and Body Mass Index." ISER Discussion Paper No. 732, March 2009. Available at SSRN: http://ssrn.com/abstract=1357093

Jeffrey, R.H., and R.H. Arnott. "Is Your Alpha Big Enough to Cover Its Taxes? The Active Management Dichotomy." *Journal of Portfolio Management* 19, no. 3 (Spring 1993): 15–25.

Kotlikoff, Laurence J., and Scott Burns. *Spend 'Till the End: The Revolutionary Guide to Raising Your Living Standard Today and When You Retire*. Simon and Schuster, 2008.

Kraft, Holger, and Claus Munk. "Optimal Housing, Consumption, and Investment Decisions over the Life-Cycle." (December 11, 2008). EFA 2008 Athens Meetings Paper. Available at SSRN: http://ssrn.com/abstract=1101468.

Liedtke, Patrick M. "From Bismarck's Pension Trap to the New Silver Workers of Tomorrow: Reflections on the German Pension Problem," European Papers on the New Welfare 4, no. 18 (February 2006).

Lleras, Miguel P. *Investing in Human Capital: A Capital Markets Approach to Student Funding*. Cambridge: Cambridge University Press, 2004.

Lusardi, Annamaria, and Peter Tutano. "Debt Literacy, Financial Experience and Overindebtedness." National Bureau of Economic Research Working Paper 14808, March 2009.

Marshall, Alfred. *Principles of Economics* (8th ed.). London: Macmillan Press, 1920.

Mawani, A., M. A. Milevsky, and K. Panyagometh. "The Impact of Personal Income Taxes on Returns and Rankings of Canadian Equity Mutual Funds." *The Canadian Tax Journal* 51, no. 2 (2003): 863–901.

Milevsky, Moshe A. *Are You a Stock or a Bond? Create Your Own Pension Plan for a Secure Financial Future*. Upper Saddle River, N.J.: Pearson Education FT Press, 2008.

_____. *Lifecycle Wealth and Risk Management: Strategic Financial Planning from Cradle to Grave*. Cambridge University Press (U.K.), to be published, 2010.

_____, and S.D. Promislow. "Florida's Pension Election: From Defined Benefit to Defined Contribution and Back." *Journal of Risk and Insurance* 71, no. 3 (2004): 381–404.

Miller, D.L, M.E. Page, A.H. Stevens, and M. Filipski. "Why Are Recessions Good for Your Health?" *American Economic Review* 99, no. 2 (2009): 122–127.

Mincer, Jacob. *Schooling, Experience and Earnings*. New York: Columbia University Press, 1974.

North Dakota State Economic Brief, vol. 17 (no. 10), October 2008.

Oyer, P. "The Making of an Investment Banker: Stock Market Shocks, Career Choice and Lifetime Income." *Journal of Finance* 63, no. 6 (December 2008): 2601–2628.

Panis, Constantijn W.A. "Annuities and Retirement Satisfaction." The RAND Corporation. Labor and Population Program, Working Paper Series 03-17. April 2003.

Pension Benefit Guaranty Corporation. *Pension Insurance Data Book 2007*. Pension Benefit Guaranty Corporation, Winter 2008. Available at http://www.pbgc.gov/docs/2007databook.pdf.

Pierlot, James. "A Pension in Every Pot: Better Pensions for More Canadians." C.D. Howe Institute Commentary (Pension Papers) no. 275, November 2008.

Plassman, B.L., et al. "Prevalence of Dementia in the United States: The Aging, Demographics and Memory Study." *Neuroepidemiology* 29 (2007):125–132.

"Quebec's Demography: The Cradle's Costly Revenge." *The Economist*, January 10, 2009.

Reed, Matthew. "Student Debt and the Class of 2007." The Project on Student Debt, October 2008. http://projectonstudentdebt.org/.

Reichenstein, W. "Tax Aware Investing: Implications for Asset Allocation, Asset Location, and Stock Management Style." *Journal of Wealth Management* 7, no. 3 (2004).

Rick, Scott, Deborah A. Small, and Eli Finkel. "Fatal (Fiscal) Attraction: Spendthrifts and Tightwads in Marriage." February 27, 2009. Available at SSRN: http://ssrn.com/abstract=1339240.

"Risk Aversion: The Bonds of Time." *The Economist*, January 10, 2009.

Sinn, H.W. "The Pay-as-You Go Pension System as Fertility Insurance and an Enforcement Device." *Journal of Public Economics* 88 (2004): 1335–1357.

Smith, Adam. *The Wealth of Nations: Complete and Unabridged.* New York: Random House, 2000.

"Smooth Operators." Review of *Portfolios of the Poor,* by Daryl Collins, Johnathan Morduch, Stuart Rutherford, and Orlanda Ruthven. *The Economist*, May 14, 2009.

Stango, V., and J. Zinman. "What Do Consumers Really Pay on Their Checking and Credit Card Accounts? Explicit, Implicit and Avoidable Costs." *American Economic Review* 99, no. 2 (2009): 424–429.

Statistics Canada. *Earnings of Canadians: Making a Living in the New Economy*. 2001 Census analysis series. Ottawa: March 11, 2003.

_____. "The Daily: University Tuition Fees." Thursday, October 9, 2008.

_____. *The Wealth of Canadians: An Overview of the Results of the Survey of Financial Security 2005*. Ottawa: Pensions and Wealth Surveys Section, Income Statistics Division, December 2006.

Streitfeld, David. "The Pain of Selling a Home for Less Than the Loan." *New York Times*, September 18, 2008.

Tamagno, Edward. *Occupational Pension Plans in Canada: Trends in Coverage and the Incomes of Seniors*. Ottawa: Caledon Institute of Social Policy, 2006.

Thaler, Richard. "Mental Accounting Matters," *Journal of Behavioral Decision Making* 12 (1999): 183–206.

Thaler, Richard H., and Cass R. Sunstein. *Nudge: Improving Decisions About Health, Wealth and Happiness*. New Haven, Conn.: Yale University Press, 2008.

Warner, J.T., and S. Pleeter. "The Personal Discount Rate: Evidence from Military Downsizing Programs." *American Economic Review* 91, no. 1 (2001): 33–53.

Yamashita, T. (2008). "Keeping up with the Joneses in McMansions: Changes in Wealth Inequality between College and High School Graduates." Portland: Reed College, Working Paper.

Yao, R., and H.H. Zhang. "Optimal Life-Cycle Asset Allocation with Housing as Collateral." Working Paper, University of North Carolina, Chapel Hill, March 2004.

_____. "Optimal Consumption and Portfolio Choices with Risky Housing and Borrowing Constraints." *The Review of Financial Studies* 18, no. 1 (2005): 197–239.

Zweig, Jason. "Does Stock Market Data Really Go Back 200 Years?" *Wall Street Journal*, July 11, 2009.

INDEX

W–Z

FINANCIAL TIMES

In an increasingly competitive world, it is quality
of thinking that gives an edge—an idea that opens new
doors, a technique that solves a problem, or an insight
that simply helps make sense of it all.

We work with leading authors in the various arenas
of business and finance to bring cutting-edge thinking
and best-learning practices to a global market.

It is our goal to create world-class print publications
and electronic products that give readers
knowledge and understanding that can then be
applied, whether studying or at work.

To find out more about our business
products, you can visit us at www.ftpress.com.